BEING AT
YOUR BEST
WHEN YOUR
KIDS ARE
AT THEIR
WORST

BEING AT YOUR BEST WHEN YOUR KIDS ARE AT THEIR WORST

Practical Compassion in Parenting

Kim John Payne, M.ED.

SHAMBHALA
Boulder
2019

Shambhala Publications, Inc.
4720 Walnut Street
Boulder, Colorado 80301
www.shambhala.com

9 8 7 6 5 4 3 2 1

First Edition
Printed in the United States of America

♾ This edition is printed on acid-free paper that meets the
American National Standards Institute Z39.48 Standard.
♻ Shambhala Publications makes every effort to print on recycled paper.
Shambhala Publications is distributed worldwide by
Penguin Random House, Inc., and its subsidiaries.

Designed by Greta D. Sibley

Library of Congress Cataloging-in-Publication Data
Names: Payne, Kim John, author.
Title: Being at your best when your kids are at their worst:
practical compassion in parenting / Kim John Payne.
Description: First Edition. | Boulder: Shambhala, 2019.
Identifiers: LCCN 2018041045 | ISBN 9781611802146 (hardback)
Subjects: LCSH: Parenting. | Child rearing. | Parent and child. |
BISAC: FAMILY & RELATIONSHIPS / Parenting / General. |
PSYCHOLOGY / Developmental / Child.
Classification: LCC HQ755.8 P39932 2019 | DDC 306.874—dc23
LC record available at https://lccn.loc.gov/2018041045

To Almuth and Annie,
my deep gratitude for your quiet support and
belief in what we do to care for
family life and for the countless children
whose lives you have gently touched
over many years.

Contents

PART TWO • THE KEY

The Compassionate Response Practice

PART THREE • THE TRANSFORMATION

The Gift of the Real You

Introduction

No parent plans to get angry—it just happens. Afterward we usually feel awful about what took place. But what is it like to live in a home where a parent's frustration regularly boils over? Here is a story recounted by an adult looking back at their childhood and the knowledge they gained from the unpredictable environment they navigated. Even though the circumstances described are harsh, it may help us to see through the eyes of a child. You'll hear the story of this ten-year-old as they try to make sense of their own parent struggling with emotional self-regulation.

A Child's View

My mother suffered with some health issues that understandably kept her from being able to keep up with the demands of life. She moved with difficulty, frustration, and pain. I can barely imagine, in retrospect, how she struggled to raise us kids, as well as be an attentive wife and the main caregiver for her own elderly parents.

She had high standards for herself, her children, and every other aspect of her life. She could be quite creative when figuring out how to keep up her homemaking ideals in spite of her debilitating condition. I remember coming home one day to see her vacuuming the floor with the hose taped to her walker. Good idea, but it meant she had to walk backward and forward dozens of times throughout the entire house to get every speck off the carpet. It must have been painful and exasperating, but she got the job done.

When we finally convinced her, decades later, to allow us to hire a professional cleaner, it only made things worse. She insisted on cleaning every last inch of the home before she could let the woman through the door. It wasn't that she was obsessive. This was just how she kept up appearances. Many women of her generation shared this trait.

Nevertheless, there was a dark side to her struggles. She often became enraged and directed her anger toward me. I have no doubt the contrary child I probably was, exasperated her and often tested her patience as she met the many responsibilities of her daily work. But some of my most vivid childhood memories involve being strapped with a thick leather belt. This was not an unusual punishment for kids in those days. When this happened I would float somewhat out of my body, see her contorted face, and even look with wonder and an almost eerie calm at the whole scene. But the hurtful sting of her words when she told me what a horrible child I was, how my future was going to be hopeless, cut more deeply than the bite of the strap.

This treatment finally ended when I was ten years old and able to stand up for myself. One day I triggered her (by doing something I can't even remember, but it must have been provocative), and as she reached for the belt, I looked her straight in the eye and said, "If you hit me again, I will hit you back just as hard. After that you will never see me again." And, in my own ten-year-old imagination, I meant it. I'd made elaborate plans to move in with a kind relative and had money for a bus ticket and a packed bag hidden and at the ready. Of course, I didn't hit her—thank goodness—but my threat shocked her, and she cried. Weirdly, I felt bad for upsetting her. The hitting stopped after that, and the shouting and shaming lessened, but a gulf between us opened up.

I have often wondered whether my mother suffered from rage that once released, could not be controlled. I have heard a definition of addiction as being "an increasing and compulsive tendency to avoid, pain, boredom, silence, inner development, and moral responsibility by displacing it with outer stimulation."

Rage can most certainly be "taking it *out*" on someone else—a clear form of outer stimulation. In my mother's case, her verbal and physical aggression may have helped her avoid facing that something was not right in her life. A person who shouts loudly enough, blames and shames others long enough, is probably trying to avoid having to face his or her own demons.

After these outbursts took place, little was said. It was as if nothing had occurred. It would make any child wonder, "Did that really happen?" Like so many other children in these kinds of situations, it never occurred to me to tell anybody about what was going on. And as odd as it may sound, I would have settled for even a small signal that she was sorry for her outbursts. A brief and gentle touch afterward that suggested remorse and a wish to reconnect would have meant everything. It never came. And as a result, our relationship floundered, which lasted into my adult years.

When I became a parent I was forced to confront my own emotions. It surprised me how little was needed to tip frustration over into anger. And I most certainly did not want to dwell there. I began to grasp my mother's parenting struggles, and slowly, over time, I developed the ability to understand what prompted her hurtful words and actions. I wish those years of harshness had never happened. But the silver lining was that I experienced what it's like to be in the presence of an adult who could not control her emotions, as she would have liked to. Most importantly, it planted in my heart the determination to do whatever I could to not go down that angry road. It also helped me realize the absolute necessity of making relational repairs when things go wrong and the cost when this does not happen.

I have heard it said, "You can't give what you did not get." In other words, if my parent was not there for me, I cannot be there for my kids. But I don't see it that way. When our babies are born and first placed in our arms, we are not thinking about our past and what we did not get. The unspoken challenge right in that moment is to begin to find capacities in ourselves that we probably never knew we had to stay present and to keep showing up to love this little, vulnerable child even when he or she pushes us and we have to reach deep inside to find caring and protecting capacities we never knew we possessed.

Building the Ark before the Flood

Have you ever found yourself in a situation in which your kid has pushed your buttons and you begin to lose it? You can hear yourself, but there seems no way to stop. The frustrated, forceful voice you are using with your child comes out of some strange "stress regress." You hear yourself speaking just like your mother or father did when they were having a rough time with you as a kid. Back then you swore you'd never talk to your own kids like that when you grew up.

But here you are, using the same words in the same steely tone. And as if seeing yourself act this way were not bad enough, you are now both mad at your kids *and* angry with yourself. You secretly wish someone would step in and rescue you. But if a friend or partner does try to intercede, you snap, "I'm fine! Would you leave me alone?"

This is the action-reaction cycle of emotional habits, which leaves parent and child filled with anger and shame in family homes across the world. Your kids do or say something that is edgy. You remind them that it is unacceptable and ask them to stop. Rather than quit, they either deflect or ignore you, and they may even ramp it up a bit. You hold it together for a while, but you can feel that red mist rising. The irritation boils over, and you react. Now you have their attention, but you also get that awful feeling that everything is speeding up and this is not going to be good.

What if there was a way to break this cycle? What if you could shift the entrenched feelings of antipathy that arise toward your child, who seems to have an unerring ability to trigger you? Wouldn't it be a relief to know that right at the moment tension begins, you had the capacity to find your own voice and stand on firm ground rather than acting out unresolved issues from your own biography?

The good news: there is a way to achieve this. As most parents know, charged confrontations blow up fast in a family. A positive alternative would have to kick in right when things are starting to escalate. And it needs to develop into an emotional muscle memory, to become a new reflex that communicates to a child that you are coming from a different place—a space in which you have become centered, firm, and loving, even when your child is being reckless and provoking you.

Making the Repairs

Life happens, conflicts flare up, and at times we lose it. Our frustration boils over, and we say or do something that comes out of anger. No matter how justified the words, the way that we spoke them does not feel right.

This is just not the kind of parent we want to be. You wish the scene had not happened, but it did. Rather than getting stuck in shame and enduring hours or even days of hurt feelings and awkward silences, by using the practices set out in this book you will be able to quickly settle yourself down. They will allow you to integrate your frustrations, get in touch with your caring and balanced self, and, crucially, make the repair with your child within a short span of time, so that the day and your relationship get back on track.

Breaking Free of Parenting Highs and Lows

The parenthood journey leads us to the heights and depths of emotional experience. Rebounding between these extremes is inevitable and even bearable, for a short while. But it's not sustainable. When living through these highs and lows, we may begin to feel that all we are doing is surviving—reacting to whatever each day throws our way. How can we develop the capability to find a firm (and fun) middle ground when life is overwhelming us?

What comes at us as parents will be unpredictable. But we can control *how* and *where* we meet these situations. It is possible to break our patterns of emotional compression and recoil, action and reaction. And although it may sound counterintuitive, the way to begin is by looking at our parenting trigger points and befriending the feelings of frustration and inadequacy that so disorient us.

We also need to be able to pause and acknowledge that we often get it right. We can lift ourselves up by remembering that things can go well and that we can be funny, loving, and even brilliant with our kids.

The early chapters of *Being at Your Best When Your Kids Are at Their Worst* will shed light on the most common ways parents get provoked. I will suggest practical strategies that deal directly with provocative situations and help us understand what issues are percolating just under the surface and binding us to a nasty cycle.

The book will then focus in on the Compassionate Response Practice, which gently but powerfully opens up and broadens the pathways within us, leading us to the acceptance that we can be frustrated *and* fabulous—that both are perfectly okay. It is called a "practice" because that is just what it is. We work at it. We prepare for the inevitable times in family life when things don't go well. The practice helps you remove old, unwanted emotional clutter and allows you to tune in to your intuition. By connecting to your inner voice, you will find that the words you speak to your child can come from a place of greater compassion and clarity.

After all, it's not just the fun things we do with our children that help build healthy relationships. How we handle the storms and struggles is what will ultimately define us in the eyes of our kids.

We Are Always Holding Our Kids— It's a Matter of How

A parent once said to me, "When my kids are not doing well, I really struggle. I don't know when to step in and sort things out and when to step back to let them work things through. As a result I feel hesitant, and my kids pick up on that."

Focusing on these two options—whether to step in or step back—is too limiting an approach. Instead, we want to shift the way we look at how to respond to flash-point moments by recognizing that we are always holding our kids emotionally. Sometimes we have a light touch and can give them space to work things out because they are doing well. But at other times we need to draw them near and hold them close so they can feel the security of our boundaries and the warmth of our support.

Most of the time we are just getting on with our family days.

In these moments our holding should be moderate in nature. But this middle ground alternative is a good place from which to tighten up or provide more space as the need arises.

Finding Your Own Voice

The heart-based strategies in *Being at Your Best When Your Kids Are at Their Worst* opens up a much wider range of responses than we might be accustomed to and helps us avoid four classic misguided parenting strategies.

1. It offers us a way out of anxiety-driven helicopter parenting, in which we hover over our kids and create too much turbulence.
2. It helps us avoid tentatively leaving them to it, which so often creates unintended disconnection.
3. It gives us ways to avoid jumping in with both boots on, a forceful approach our kids can perceive as threatening or overreactive.
4. It provides us with a practical way to observe what's happening and confidently determine whether to hold a situation firmly or moderately or decide that a soft touch is all that's needed.

When we become confident that we often strike the right tone with our struggling kids (or at least one that is not wildly discordant), we thicken and strengthen the bonds of our relationship. Trust builds. Rather than push us away when they are disoriented and frustrated, our kids will lean into us, because they know we are a safe emotional harbor, a place where they can rest and regroup.

When They Are Angry, They Are Vulnerable

Although this book is called *Being at Your Best When Your Kids Are at Their Worst*, what we as parents want above all is to be at our most loving when our kids are at their most vulnerable. When a child, tween, or teen becomes deeply angry and upset, the layers of their being peel back, exposing deeper needs and sensitivities. It is at this very moment that what we say and do really matters, because it will penetrate right to their inner being. This is why our most vivid childhood memories are often about difficult times we suffered through and how our parents handled those things—roughly or with sensitivity and care.

The overriding aim of *Being at Your Best* is to help you to find balance and create a safe place for *you and your child* to pause and reorient during these defining parenting moments.

Practically, you will see that this book is presented in three sections. Part 1 explores the derailments that prevent you from being the parent you want to be. We will look at what may be triggering you to get stuck within old, unwanted action-reaction habits with your kids. Part 2 takes a deep dive into the Compassionate Response Practice, which is a visualization and meditation that powerfully works to integrate your frustrations and struggles with a child's behavior that is pressing your buttons while encouraging you not to forget that you can be a kind, caring, funny, and competent parent. Part 3 details the transformative outcomes you can experience in finding your own calm, competent voice. What you will read in these chapters is less a traditional self-help book and more a map to a journey within yourself, where you can find a place in which you feel good about your parenting on a day-to-day basis. As your kids grow up and out into the world, you will have a feeling that you have done a solid job and that your overarching hope for them will be achieved: that they will be okay.

PART ONE

THE PROBLEM

*What Gets in the Way of
Being at Our Best?*

In this section we look at what pushes our buttons and why. We will explore:

- How we can be on the family dance floor but also, at the same time, on the objective balcony
- Our reactive habits (or what I call *repetitive emotional strain injuries*) and how to heal them
- What your body-based response to family tensions can tell you
- How conflict avoidance (or *harmony addiction*) and other responses we have to challenging family situations may have their roots in our own upbringing

- The reasons our kids test us out and push us
- Feeling unseen and undervalued, and practical strategies to establish appreciation
- How the four pillars of simplifying family life can create more calm and balance in day-to-day life when it all gets to be too much
- How to target what is within your influence to change and staying close to your family values

I

The Balcony and the Playground

My students pulled open the door to the little shed. "Yes," they shouted, "it's a *really* big tangle!" The rope they stared at was no ordinary rope. It was bright orange and a couple of hundred yards long. We used it to mark out our play area for games class. I'd learned early on in my teaching career that some elementary-age kids playing tag would rather run to the next town than get caught. So marking a boundary was a professional necessity. My colleague also used the rope but often ran out of time at lesson's end and, rather than store it neatly, dumped it into the shed in a spectacular, tangled mess.

So my class became expert at the art of untangling. In fact, they looked forward to it! They even timed themselves to see how quickly they could do it. They devised two ways to go about it. For the first, we'd send a couple of children up to the tower attached to the schoolhouse building. This little tower had a balcony from which you could get a great view of the playground. The kids would look down and, from their bird's-eye view, call out helpful instructions to the scrum of untanglers below.

The second detangling trick the children learned was *never pull on a knot*. If you do so, the rope gets badly matted and becomes nearly impossible to use. Instead, they made sure to open each tangle up to create more and more space. With time and effort, the jumble unraveled, and the children would let out a triumphant collective hoot. The kids called this chore—which they had transformed into a fun activity—the Knotty Game.

A BEING AT YOUR BEST TOOL
The Tangle and Tensions of Emotions

The metaphors of the kids' untangling techniques are striking. We can apply these same simple principles to all of our relationships and, in particular, to parenting situations. When we find ourselves in a tangle of emotions with our kids, what to do?

Step One:
Climb the Tower and Get Out on the Balcony

First of all, we need some objectivity—not easy to find, I know, but essential. It's helpful to climb up into our own parenting tower, stand on the balcony, and witness what is playing out. What needs are not being met that are causing tensions to flare up?

This does not mean we detach ourselves from the activity below. Instead, we can guide it with a more expansive perspective. From that vantage point, we can be more helpful. We can identify a snarl that may be forming and call down instructions, rather than blindly make a mess of a situation and not be able to do anything about it. As one mother of three children put it, "What helps is that my thinking and observations can influence what I am doing before things get out of control."

Here is a practical way to stand on the balcony without signaling to a child or teen that you are disconnected and aloof.

Connect: "I can see this is hard for us."
Altering your first response changes the direction of an exchange with your kids. Opening a conversation with an "I can see . . ." statement sends the message that you have been watching. It also reassures everyone that you are not getting angry. Most importantly, it subtly reinforces to your child that you are a loving family.

Here are a few other examples:

"I can see this is not going so well."
"I can see this really bothers you."
"I can see that you probably need some space now. We can find out what is bothering you a little later."

Step Two:

On the Playground, Opening the Tangle

It is so easy to get entangled in blame and frustration. That's when we tug too hastily on the ropes and feel constricted. The more we pull, the tighter a situation knots up, until our family ends up in a matted, restrictive mess. Any possible solution to the problem gets lost in a snarl of misunderstanding and anger. What we need to do instead is open up space in the knots.

Get their perspective:

"Can you help me understand how you see it?"

The *truth* of any situation is a journey, not a destination. Kids have their own perspectives on how a hard situation has come about. Too often we presume how we see something is the way it is. As adults we tend to be more objective and grasp more of the bigger picture than our kids, but we can parent more effectively when we pause and ask them for their viewpoint. It's always better to hear them out first, rather than jumping into problem-solving mode.

The question I like to ask is:

"Can you help me understand how you see it?"
If there are two or three people involved, you can add,

"The way you see it is probably different from how
your brothers or I do. That is normal and fine."

If it is just you and your child in a muddle, explain that seeing things differently is normal. It helps you both maintain your truth and stay connected to your child because by allowing different perspectives, you are promoting mutual respect. If siblings are involved, it's common for them to battle to gain your allegiance, and things can escalate quickly. Using the second statement stops them from trying to recruit you over to their side by insisting they are the only one telling the truth and the other siblings are lying.

Change your tone: It is not what *is said but the* way *it is spoken.* The two strategies above—"I can see . . ." and "Can you help me understand . . . ?"—help take the edge off your tone, which your kids are so sensitive to. Most of all, it helps you, in a very practical way, shift to a different place within yourself. Rather than falling into an all-to-familiar escalation pattern, you can stand on that objective balcony and, at the same time, engage with your kids at the playground level.

It was endearing to watch the kids struggle and work things through in the Knotty Game. Even though they knew that pulling on a knot did not work, some children could not resist doing it. Each time that happened, someone would say, "Don't pull, it only makes it worse" or "Give it more space."

One nine-year-old girl called out, "Don't choke it! Let it breathe." That's exactly what we aim to do when we coach ourselves to observe ourselves and our family from the tower balcony while engaging lovingly with them in the playground at the same time.

2

Healing a Repetitive Emotional Strain Injury

A strong parallel can be made between how we treat problem areas in our bodies and how we can best work with the emotional bruises of day-to-day parenting. Physical or occupational therapists typically treat a problem area in two ways. First they try to determine what repetitive action is causing muscle inflammation or wear and tear on the joints. When particular repeated movements have become a bad habit—known as a *movement blind spot*—they need to be corrected if the body is to heal. Second, therapists massage the surrounding area to relax adjacent muscles, rather than pushing and poking the injured spot itself—which would hurt too much and likely cause additional inflammation. They do this to keep the tension from spreading and to create a more relaxed space so that the inflammation can dissipate.

In our family relationships we often have behavioral blind spots, things we do over and over that cause emotional inflammation. By becoming aware of these bad habits, we can begin to understand the cause of the pain and contemplate changes we might make.

Here are three examples of bad habits we can bring to light:

- provocative or sarcastically tinged communication styles
- unintended put-downs
- overly assertive questioning

Though we may not interact with our children in these ways intentionally, they will nonetheless respond to such patterned behavior by becoming defiant or withdrawn. I call these reactions *push back or fall back.* We have triggered in them a need to protect themselves from us.

When we repeatedly poke at a problem situation with a family member, we cause emotional irritation to flare up. Granted, our kids' behaviors can be annoying at times—especially when they do the same thing over and over. But getting frustrated and forcefully telling a child, "You are acting like a baby" or "You are the oldest and you should know better" simply escalates the tension. You and your child have clearly developed a relationship sore spot. Rather than prod at it, try to create space around it. A subtle shift in your emotional reflexes can produce remarkable results.

When author and business marketing expert David Levin looks at campaigns he has implemented that did not go as well as he expected, he resists the temptation to dump everything and start again. Instead, he says, "Most often what I need to do is figure out what I didn't see and make a tiny two-degree directional change. Then so often everything begins to flow properly."

The same can be true with parenting. If we can find out where we need to make those little two-degree pivots and implement them, we can open up healthier pathways to connecting in our families.

A BEING AT YOUR BEST TOOL
Fever-Based Sensitivity

Our kids are so attuned to us that little is needed to breathe more space into our relationships with them. This is particularly true if your connection with your child has become *emotionally fevered*. They are already on high alert, so any positive change you make will be perceived immediately and quickly produce de-escalation. After all, everyone wants to be relaxed and feel safe.

It may take time to heal, but a shift is definitely under way. As one dad with two teenagers confided, "I'd got into the habit of making sarcastic comments, like, 'Oh, here we go again.' I didn't *mean it* as a put-down, and it seemed a lot better than shouting. But my kids reacted badly to it every time. I kept justifying my reaction by telling my wife, 'Well, they start it.' 'You sound like a child,' she would reply, which didn't lead to a great conversation either. The moment I showed a flicker of self-restraint and shifted my attitude, something amazing happened: when I said, 'Okay. Tell me what's bugging you about this,' they just opened up, like they'd been waiting forever for me to quit going at them."

We will go more deeply into how to avoid *pulling on a knot* or *poking at a sore spot* in part 2 of this book, which explores the Compassionate Response Practice in detail. However, you can use what you have just read as an emotional early warning detection system right now. Here's how it works.

A BEING AT YOUR BEST TOOL
The Clench

We often sense when a problem or an argument is coming. Disagreements smolder and build up over time. But even when they flare up quickly, we have a few seconds to *brace for impact*. Many people describe a clenching feeling they get when they sense a fight coming on. It's an instinctual human reaction. One mother told me it's "like being squeezed—but not at all in a good way."

The next time you are headed into an argument with your partner or kids, pause for a moment and consider what form your clenching takes. Try as best you can to climb up onto that balcony and see yourself and how you react. Notice where in your body you feel the clench and the qualities it has. For example, you may feel your shoulders raise and tighten, or maybe your hands ball up into fists. Some parents have mentioned they feel a tightening in their throat and as a result their voice feels and sounds constricted. Personally, I notice that I tend to lock my knees in a "brace-for-impact" type of stance. If that is too hard to do in the moment, then mull it over afterward.

If you can motivate yourself to perform this self-check, something small but significant can happen. Just like the occupational therapist who identifies what physical action is stressing a problem area, you are shining a spotlight on an unconscious emotional habit. You won't be able to completely change your reactions every time, but you will likely be able to de-escalate situations more often. The more your awareness increases, the greater your chances of avoiding *repetitive emotional strain injuries.*

Most often, our body's physical reaction to a stressful situation comes first, and words flood in second. Yes, things happen quickly, but it is possible to train yourself to note when your body starts to lock itself into a clenching pattern. This can serve as a warning signal that provocative words are about to come out of your mouth. The brain science is pretty clear. The moment you go into your *observing brain*, you can override your *fight-or-flight brain*. The small pause you create is all-important to your ability to break free of old, unhealthy emotional habits.

In a nutshell, you have just set up an early warning system that will help keep you from overtaxing a small group of emotional muscles. Instead, your parenting exchanges will be carried out by a much wider range of emotional muscles. And at the end of the day, as you lie down in bed, you'll feel tired but pleased by a family day well lived.

3

Derailments from the Past

STUFF ACCUMULATES

Most of the time family life just chugs along the tracks of daily
life. The train slows at steep inclines—where certain issues need
to be worked through— then picks up pace, regaining its regular
rhythm. But when things happen too quickly, family life can
feel like it's headed off the rails. Derailment can be dangerous.
People can get hurt. And when all forward movement ceases, it
takes a lot of heavy lifting to get the family back on track.

In the next four chapters we will explore the most common
causes of family derailments. It should come as no surprise that
some are triggered by material from our unresolved past, some

by reactions to what is happening at present, and others by anxieties about the future our kids are heading toward.

We can often sense when the tensions beneath our interactions are building up. Identifying and understanding these unwanted cycles of action-reaction can help us avoid family derailments. Perhaps not every section on derailment in *Being at Your Best When Your Kids Are at Their Worst* will strike a chord with you. But when a chord *is* struck, pause, put the book down, and try to carry your realization into your day.

Finding Places to Put Stuff

Stuff accumulates, especially the kinds of things that don't have a place in which to be kept organized. We see that untidy thing out of place, and because we don't have a better option, we tend to leave it there. We might have a vague sense of annoyance that it continues to hang around, getting in the way day after day. Or we might pick it up and walk around with it for a while and then put it down in another place where it doesn't really belong.

The interesting thing here is that this description could be true for either a piece of dirty laundry or an unresolved emotion. The question is, why does this happen? First, as I just mentioned, often we don't have anywhere specific to put it. And second, even if there is a place, unless it is within reach, it is easier in a busy life just to leave the thing where it is. Either way, the out-of-place thing is going to leave you feeling frustrated and your space, cluttered.

Stuff Attracts Stuff

Have you ever noticed that when one item does not have a place or is not put away where it belongs, it tends to attract other lost or discarded things? Some strange magnetic force seems to be at work. Your kids have a sixth sense about the unconscious or unresolved places in your home *and in your psyche*. They will dump their unwashed emotional laundry in a pile right beside yours. Soon you have a growing pile of unattractive stuff.

The outcome? We move from a generalized wish that things could be a little tidier to a growing annoyance that an accumulating mess is being ignored. This finally morphs into a rage-tinged flurry of activity because "we have had enough!" In the end we can become overwhelmed by the unresolved emotional clutter that closes in on us.

"If It's Hysterical, It's Historical"

In truth, it is not only the accumulating stuff that causes anger but also our frustration at our lack of inner organization to deal with it. When singer-songwriter Jewel introduced me to the quote "If it's hysterical, it's historical," from Melody Beattie's book *The Language of Letting Go*, I realized the phrase perfectly encapsulates how disproportionate our emotionally charged outbursts can be to the situations that trigger them. Most of our intense, historically unresolved feelings originate in our childhood and teen years. But issues that haven't been dealt with in our adult life can also cause outsized outbursts, which bewilder and spook our kids. They become wary of us and distance themselves, triggering even more problematic parental behavior. In this way a discouraging cycle of discord develops.

The first step we can take toward breaking this cycle is to explore the unresolved experiences we are holding on to and the way in which we see them. At its core the Compassionate Response Practice requires that we recognize and sift through the unconscious emotions, but not in a big and generalized way. Instead, our aim is more modest. We narrow the aperture of the lens we are looking through to focus on what influences from the past might be playing into our parenting.

As one father wrote, "My mother was the supercontrolling kind who never really listened to me. I hated it. When my own kids didn't listen to me about relatively little things . . . kaboom! I would get weirdly angry. When I realized that I was playing out an old, painful loop from my childhood, it helped me understand that shouting at my kids wouldn't get them to listen to me. I was just repeating the same behavior that had shut down much of my relationship with my mother."

Harmony Addiction

The pursuit of happiness is like a waking anxiety dream in which the object of our compulsive chase keeps disappearing around the next corner, remaining tantalizingly out of reach. We need to guard against *harmony addiction*, in which we strive for rainbow-colored, aura-balancing family experiences daily. Where joy is *good* and struggle is seen as *bad*. Everyone knows that an idealized picture of family life where everyone is happy and contented all the time is a mirage, and yet the desire to achieve it lies deep within us.

We need to remind ourselves that we do not become happy with how things are going in our family by rejecting the parts of ourselves that we don't like, even though it's tempting to think that we can dump these feelings into a landfill of unwanted emotions and failed parenting experiments.

How Past Patterns Distort Present Parenting

Two main patterns from our past can cause discomfort when we encounter parenting conflicts. The first is manifest if we come from a home in which the prevailing spoken—or unspoken—principle was "We do not *do* conflict." In families like these, tensions were tamped down quickly and thoroughly and never allowed to surface and bubble over. The second pattern involves the frequent outward expression of indiscriminate, undirected, downright scary anger. As children, we are simply overwhelmed. We don't know how to cope with such raw emotions, nor do we have the authority to handle them.

Both these extremes can trigger the following patterns in our own parenting:

- Conflict becomes associated with lack of safety.
- We don't learn de-escalation strategies.
- We retreat from intense emotions.
- Old, destructive hurt-feeling patterns persist, sometimes for decades, because they have not been properly worked through.
- We become uncomfortable when our kid is upset and get angry at our child for getting angry.
- We lump all intense emotions into the avoidance basket and miss opportunities to solve problems when they are small and still easy to handle.
- We come to associate anger with deeper feelings of powerlessness.

We run the risk of repeating the patterns listed above with our own kids and creating either *generational conflict aversion* or—at the other end of the spectrum—*anger justification*.

When we claim we were raised in a family in which "we just told the brutal truth," we are in the throes of anger justification. I remember hearing this exact statement from a dad who came to me for counseling with his wife. He sought help because he was prone to unpredictable outbursts of rage. I asked his permission to speak with him as pointedly as possible. He nodded. So I said, in a clear and straightforward (and I hope kind) way, "There is a world of difference between speaking the brutal truth and speaking the truth brutally." It sunk in—and that conversation became a turning point in our work together.

If we engage in the Compassionate Response Practice with energy, effort, and sincerity, transformations such as the one my client underwent are possible. As long as we can learn to avoid harmony addiction and embrace the tensions that are a natural part of living and growing together, we can realistically experience a healthy flow of happiness in our family life.

4

Derailments from the Past

INHERITED AND DISINHERITED
PARENTING STYLES

It's normal and healthy to see aspects of ourselves in our children. Seeing our own physical characteristics and behavioral
mannerisms mirrored back to us is in part what bonds us to
our son or daughter. And it can certainly be endearing, cute,
infuriating, embarrassing, or just plain funny to watch as our
kids move or speak *just like us*. However, it's not helpful or
healthy when our own childhood backgrounds get tangled
up with our responses and reactions as we parent our kids.
Enmeshment occurs when our own life history—and especially
our unresolved issues—get all jumbled with our child's experiences to the degree that it is no longer possible to separate the
two. This can express itself in some unhelpful ways.

- It can prevent us from really hearing what our kids are trying to tell us.
- It can prompt us to jump to conclusions about what is happening and to give advice that makes things worse.
- It discourages our kids from disclosing to us what is happening in their lives, because we overreact and *make too big a deal out of everything.*
- It conveys the message that we care more about ourselves than about them.
- Our overreactions can embarrass our kids when we confront others.
- We do not model good problem solving, as our child can pick up that all these years later we have not moved on from an issue and that "something weird" is going on.

In our grandparents' days the phrase "parenting style" did not even exist. But starting at some point in the 1960s, declarations like "I don't really like all that Dr. Spock stuff" or "I used to like 1-2-3 Magic but it got a little behavior mod–ish for me" started to make their way into our collective parenting dialogue. As they searched for the best approach to handle their kids, people would say things like, "These days I prefer the Attachment Parenting approach, but when is this cosleeping thing supposed to end? Because our bedroom is getting kind of crowded" or "I tried Love and Logic, but my three-year-old did not seem to relate to all that talking, no matter how logical I was."

Our own parents may have bought into one or another of

these fads or been influenced by them without even being aware of it. But we can be certain of one thing: the way we were raised has a powerful effect on our own parenting approach, especially when things get tough.

As you read through the following parenting-style descriptions, pause and consider two main dynamics. First, identify the kind of parenting you received as a child. In doing so you begin to build a crucial understanding of the undercurrents that were at work during your childhood and that inevitably shape your present-day parenting, especially during tense moments with your spouse and kids. Second, try to recognize the parenting style you have adopted. It's good to bring this into focus and to examine it carefully, especially since it is highly likely that the way you are now raising your kids is governed, to a large degree, by your conscious *and* subconscious reactions to the way you were raised.

The Fads

Here are some of the main swings in disciplinary philosophies over the past ninety years, grouped in phases and spanning the decades when each style achieved the height of its popularity.

The parenting-style pendulum swung back and forth from a tight and strict approach to a freewheeling, more relaxed one every ten to twelve years. The freewheeling years gradually gave birth to a collective worry that parents were not giving their kids "enough guidance" and the kids were "getting out of control."

Then, after a shift back to restrictions and stern discipline, concern that parents were being "too uptight" and that their kids "were being suppressed" once again took hold.

Blind Obedience: Pre-1960s

Many of the seniors I spoke with in the 1980s and 1990s became parents during the Great Depression of the 1930s or during the Second World War. Back then, raising a family was synonymous with roll-up-your-sleeves hard work. In fact, discipline wasn't really an issue. Immediate survival and "just getting through" were much more pressing.

Everyone in the family did their part. Children either did their work properly and contributed to the family livelihood, or they didn't. If the effort was not good enough, the parental focus was on the child getting it right. There was little room for negotiation. In a nutshell, parents did not expect to be questioned, and they certainly did not feel the need to explain themselves to their children.

The Transitional Years: 1946–1969

After the postwar economic recovery and into the 1950s, parenting styles began to change. A newly stable and prosperous society was shaking itself free of old ways. Benjamin Spock was among the first to bring attention to parenting with his influential book *Baby and Child Care*. Throughout the 1950s, many in what could loosely be called the middle class took up his advice. This seemed to form the groundwork for more widespread change in the 1960s and early '70s. It was in these years that wider sections of society began to question and think critically about parenting, while others chose to write about parenting in magazines and newspapers, crossing social and economic boundaries by printing articles on family life.

Freestyling: 1970s

Perhaps because some children raised in the "Spock years" were now hitting their teens in the 1970s, young people pushed back hard against the "Do as I say, not as I do" approach. As so often happens, older siblings influence younger ones, and this new attitude seemed to spread throughout age groups. Parents felt this pressure and worried that previously accepted parenting conventions might be too cold and punitive, so they started allowing new freedoms. Mandatory chores began to disappear from the home. Parents talked about letting their kids be experimental and creative, rather than burdening them with household duties. They were perhaps reacting to the "blind obedience" world in which they themselves had been raised; kids were now allowed to discuss, negotiate, and even debate with their parents. To these more open-minded parents, a child's "no" was not a statement of intolerable defiance but rather a healthy form of self-expression.

However, by the mid-to-late 1970s, some parents began to worry that they might be giving their kids too much freedom and free expression. Kids seemed to be skirting basic levels of accountability and spinning out of control.

The Reward and Punishment Years: 1980s

Behavior modification was introduced to parenting in the late 1970s and became popularized throughout the 1980s. This was largely due to Dr. B. F. Skinner's theory of radical behaviorism, which championed a gold-star system that entailed the giving and taking away of privileges. Here was a way to haul your kids back into line.

What concerned parents about behavior modification, with its rewards and punishments, was the underlying motivation for compliance. A child raised in this context did not tend to understand and accept a parent's true authority: the youngster complied because of what he or she could get out of the exchange (the star, the reward). The system shaped kids into expert bargainers, negotiators, and cost-benefit analyzers.

The time-out, which had been around for a while, became widely used during this phase. Sometimes it was referred to as "social exclusion" or "tactical ignoring" or an "extinction procedure." Yes—those terms were actually used. But over time, parents became concerned that this punitive way of excluding a child sent the message that acceptance depended on unquestioning compliance to power and drove an emotional wedge between them and their children.

Parents Become "The Management": 1990s

Parents started moving away from behavior modification because they didn't like being prison wardens and because they saw that their kids responded by working the system to their own advantage.

So back swung the parenting pendulum—and the era of behavior management was born. In this system, the kids were a "team" and the parent, their "manager." Family discussions were no longer led by a parent. Instead, team meetings, comprised of stakeholders, were facilitated by a parent-manager. Parents may not have used these exact terms, but the books that promoted the system certainly did.

Mothers, in particular, were staying in the workforce longer than ever before—and having children later in life. Consequently, they brought home what appeared to be successful team-oriented office practices. As workforce managers, parents wanted to give their team (the kids) a healthy palette of choices.

However, kids raised in this manner often felt confused about who was really in charge. And they were frequently asked to "review" their choices well before they had the emotional maturity to do so. Or perhaps they were subjected to time-outs, which reinforced in them the concern that "if I do something you don't like, you are going to reject me and send me away."

And in collaborative situations, such as when you wanted them to help clean house, they would unionize and defy management outright by collectively doing *nothing*. The bottom line: it was awkward, *and just plain silly*, for parents to act as managers. Think about it: we cannot resign from parenthood (nor can we fire our kids)!

Raised on Praise: 2000–Present

Ever since the late 1990s—following parent-manager excesses— the pendulum has swung back to command-and-control parenting. Call it "behavior affirmation." It's subtle and appears liberal, positive, and encouraging of a child or teen. However, while it is normal and natural to affirm a child and let him know how much you appreciate his help, behavior affirmation, with its intensity and frequency, takes praise to a whole other level. Everything is labeled a "good job!" In fact, if you examine it closely, behavior affirmation is really a sugarcoated version of behavior modification, only the emphasis is placed on *praise* rather than *punishment*. Both approaches manipulate a young child— who hungers for parental attention—by controlling her with either approval and rewards or disapproval and punishments. The behavior affirmation approach is still with us and essentially provides kids with two main choices: either they actually believe they are *that good*, or they sense that the parent may be faking it. Either way, this mind-set does not translate well in adult life, since the ability to seek, accept, and act on honest feedback that is not always rosy is critical to success in life.

Explaining a Kid into Submission: 2005–Present

Some parents are serial explainers, engaging in incessant behavior justification. This style became very popular starting around 2005 and although the raised-on-praise style still continued, a new wave—maybe a quiet tsunami—of overtalking parents began to form and hit the parenting shores. There have always been moms and, even more often, dads who can't help but dive into great detail about all aspects of life. When exposed to incessant overexplanation, your child runs two risks. One is that he or she will become a nutty professor who absorbs a lot of information and morphs into an enlarged head transported by little feet. The overdevelopment of facts, figures, thinking, and analyzing in kids can come at the expense of the development of important social skills and can severely compromise the ability to make friends. Or your child or teen may shut down and tune you out. Either result hampers your relationship with your child and his or her ability to navigate social waters.

Those are brief overviews of the most influential parenting styles of recent times. For some it may be resoundingly clear which parenting fad they were subjected to as kids. For others of us it may be less so. Kids often experience contrasting parenting styles under the same roof, which could be confusing and disorienting. One mother of three young children wrote: "My mother was definitely into behavior management, although I doubt she knew the term. She would give us a ton of choices and allow us to negotiate. I'm sure she did this to be kind, but it drove my dad crazy. His version of behavior modification was a hardliner's. Privileges were often angrily revoked, and time-outs could last for hours."

A BEING AT YOUR BEST TOOL
Decision Time

Take a moment to reflect on your childhood. What was your parents' disciplinary style? Try to identify what parenting patterns governed your upbringing, how they may still be affecting you, and how you parent your own kids. When you make a concerted effort to observe your parenting inclinations, your self-awareness increases, and you are more likely to catch yourself as you drift back into inherited patterns. You may feel that some of your parents' techniques were fine and happily replicate them. However, parents often want to avoid foisting disciplinary styles on their children that they feel were inhibiting or harmful to them when they were kids. What's important here is that we pause, consider our biographical patterns, and make more conscious, informed decisions going forward.

Here's an example of a parent who made a conscious effort to grapple with biographical enmeshment. I was contacted by the father of an eleven-year-old boy, who told me what happened when his son confided to him that he was being picked on by a new teacher at school. "I hardly let my son finish before angrily declaring that his teacher had no right to do that," he recalled. "I told him I knew exactly how he felt and that I'd sort this all out right away."

The dad himself had often felt singled out by certain "mean" teachers in middle school, because he was not one of the "smart kids." Despite his rocky school years, he had grown up to become a very successful property developer who appeared confident and commanding in most social situations. But that evening, as he recalled his own belittling school-day experiences, his resentment grew, and he turned into someone he almost couldn't recognize.

The next morning the ride to school was unusually quiet. At drop-off the father—who was by now seething—got out of the car and followed his son into the classroom. He challenged the teacher disrespectfully and embarrassed his son in front of his classmates, who later told him his father had acted and spoken "really weird." The son was mortified by his dad's public display.

The father mentioned the incident to his wife, but that night at dinner, she got more details from her son, who refused to go back to school. She insisted her husband call me for a consultation.

We explored how patterns of enmeshment were clouding his actions and his connection to his son using the Compassionate Response Practice, which can help a parent disentangle his own biography from the needs of his child. The main thing he wanted was to develop a practical plan to ensure that his son felt safe in the class. Once he had calmed down, he worked with the Compassionate Response Practice for a week and to some extent separated his experiences from his son's. He was then able to go to the teacher, who was new to the class, and convey that his son was quite shy. The teacher had been calling on him during lessons because she felt that with a little encouragement, she could draw him out and he would be able to answer the questions. But the boy had interpreted this as the teacher picking on him. The dad expressed that it would probably be better for the teacher to have one-on-one conversations with his son, rather than asking him questions in front of the class. They agreed that this was a good approach, and to his credit, the father apologized to the teacher for his presumptive behavior. At home he told his son that he would be much more careful in the future.

What happened to this father is not uncommon. One of our most basic instincts is to protect our family. It's perfectly normal that when we interact with our kids, we apply what we have learned from our own lives about what can be painful. But the primal reaction is only a starting point. Think of it as first-base reflexive parenting. We need to head to second base and round third, by mustering the forces to hold back our own story. This does not mean we reject or deny our past. We simply work consciously to keep it in the background so that we can be present to hear what our child's actual experiences are, because they are unique to him or her. The dad in the story struggled to overcome his enmeshment tendency. When a situation with his child triggered him to flash on the past, he learned to allow himself a moment to objectively recognize his memory. But the recollection also became a powerful signal to step forward, listen to his son, and help him make a plan if that was possible.

In a nutshell, if a situation comes up that triggers a *backward-biography* or *stress-regress response* that we get stuck in for any more than a minute or two, we are in real danger of enmeshment. If, however, we can shift to a *now-and-future-planning mode*, we will very likely be fully present for our kids when they need us most and provide them with the support they require to adjust and thrive.

5

Derailments in the Present

We all know it's a mistake to personalize a child's bad behavior. But in the heat of the moment, we often make difficult inter-actions with our children all about us. A mother whose nine-year-old daughter was engaging in lots of outbursts and arguments confided, "I get so hurt by the things she says and the accusations she makes!" She described how unfairly she was being treated by her daughter, who seemed "to know just how to press my buttons, particular about things I am sensitive to." The woman recounted the guilt she felt about her divorce and how much she worried about being a single parent. "When my daughter says she hates me and tells me that all of her friends' moms are *soo* much nicer, it hits me where I'm most vulnerable, because I have to work long hours and I know that makes me grumpy."

This defensive mind-set is much more common than you would think. There are some things to understand about this kind of situation. First, making a difficult interaction with a child about *you* is never helpful. Of course, we all know this in the rational part of our brains, but it still happens so very often. Personalizing can lead you into a relational maze: it's easy to get lost in the twists and turns of an argument, end up wondering how this all happened, and, worst of all, find yourself standing there on your own, unable to make your way out.

Parents have told me countless times that they feel they are engaged in a battle of wills with their kids. One dad said to me that he was personally "under siege" and that he needed to defend himself from his child's behavior. I once jokingly asked a group of parents if they thought their children planned their difficult behavior. To my surprise, a good number felt their kids did. You may think yours do, too, because they are so good at triggering you, but I can assure you their behavior is decidedly subconscious, not Machiavellian. Your child, tween, or teen simply does not wake up in the morning, consider a list of things that will upset you, choose the most effective, and lie in wait for the best moment to inflict maximum hurt.

It's Not about the Truth—It's about Power

I explained to the single mom mentioned above—who felt so vulnerable to her daughter's criticism—that what matters most is not whether her daughter's words are true or hurtful, but the intensity of her own reaction and response.

I asked her if she thought other kids say these kinds of things to their parents. She was pretty sure they did. Did she think, I asked, that every parent reacts the way she did? She described an exchange she had recently witnessed when she picked up her younger son from a playdate. Her son's friend was unhappy that the visit was over and angrily exclaimed to his father, "You always make me stop playing!" Rather than react outwardly and respond irritably, the dad replied, in an upbeat tone, "You had a great time with Aaron, and now his mom is here to take him home." The little boy looked sullen but said nothing more and was soon waving good-bye to his friend as they drove away. We agreed that what the little boy said to his dad was likely to be true. But it was clear that because the father did not react to his son's jab and defend himself, his son calmed down and quickly moved on.

If child-parent arguments were about harsh-but-true comments, every parent would get upset quite often. But clearly this is not the case. The flustered mom asked me, "If the conflict isn't about the horrible things being said that make me feel guilty, what is it about?" "It's not about whether you are the nicest or meanest parent," I replied, "or whether—at that particular moment—you are loved or hated. It's about how you react and what your verbal or emotional response triggers in your child."

This mom's anger and her perceptible *need to protect herself* was not only inflaming her interactions with her daughter, it was also doing something far more worrisome—giving her child power over her. Here we have a basic human dynamic: when we feel forced to justify our actions, we are diminished. The aggressor becomes larger, and the receiver shrinks.

For example, who holds the most power in a courtroom—the person on the witness stand defending herself or the prosecuting attorney? The quickest way to put ourselves in the family court witness box is to get caught up in defending ourselves against our kids' sharp words. The most important thing to understand is that *our troubles begin when we take things personally*.

The Leadership Vacuum

If a frustrated child or teen lobs a mean comment at you and senses that you respond defensively, she will perceive a tilt in the balance of power. This does not happen on a conscious level. But she senses that you are off-center, not standing on solid ground. And, as strange as it may sound, your perceived imbalance triggers a moment of panic in your child. Basically, the boundaries she was pushing up against *in you* have given way. That lack of stability causes her to feel emotionally unsupported. She's leaned on a wall she depends on, and instead of supporting her weight, it has crumbled. She feels like she's falling, suddenly unsafe and disoriented because the person she counts on to be firm—*to be in charge*—has stepped back and even abdicated this leadership role. The child then forcefully and somewhat desperately tries to step into and occupy what she experiences as a leadership vacuum. It's crucial to understand that she does this not to rebel but in order to feel secure again.

Getting Pinged

When kids "try it out," what are they really doing? In *The Soul of Discipline* I wrote that "I have never met a willfully disobedient child, only disoriented ones." Kids send out waves of negative behavior because they feel emotionally lost. It's one of the most unsettling states a person can experience. Whom do they push up against? Us. *Their parents!* It's as if they are using a behavioral echolocation system that bounces waves of challenging actions or words off of us in order to elicit reactions. This helps them get a read on what they are feeling and reorient themselves. Navigators at sea call this "pinging," and there is not a parent alive who hasn't been thoroughly pinged.

The silver lining is that they do this to us because we are the people they trust the most. Our kids' difficult behavior is a form of communication. What's up to us is how carefully we listen and how sensitively we calibrate our reactions.

When Do We Get Pinged?

Kids ping us when they are feeling emotionally lost. It can happen when things aren't going well socially with friends and they feel like they are being overlooked. For example, if a new kid at school forms a strong, exclusive bond with a longtime friend whom your child relied on, your son is likely to feel sad, lost, and disoriented. He may well act out and ping you. But it's not because he wants to make life difficult for you; rather, it's because he feels the social ground shifting under his feet and is seeking firm ground to stand on.

A mom once asked me if pinging can take the form of withdrawal rather than challenging behavior. The answer is a definite yes. In such a case her child is not *acting out*, he's *sinking in*. Or, to put it another way, her child is *falling back* rather than *pushing back*. In both situations children need our help to find their way to being themselves.

Here are a few other reasons a child may feel lost and ping us:

- She feels misunderstood at school, not just by other kids but by the teachers and administration.
- He is overwhelmed by the amount of homework, after-school activities, and sports.
- She feels at sea without a key teacher, mentor, or advisor to help her navigate her demanding days.
- He is unable to understand what he is supposed to learn in his lessons and fears that he is failing.

Kids also act out and need to reorient themselves when big family changes are afoot, such as:

- Moving to another house
- The death of a dear family member or a beloved pet
- Financial pressures affecting the family
- Serious illness in the family

But what's most difficult for parents to pick up on is when a child pings them because he or she is undergoing developmental changes. The classic view is that physical, cognitive, and social changes occur at the ages of two, six, nine, and fourteen, and this is true for many. However, life is too rich and complicated for this pattern to be set in stone. Changes can occur at different ages for different kids.

When my daughter was fourteen, her gentle bubbliness, which we had come to love, gave way to sharp, sarcastic comments that could rattle our family interactions. At first we were puzzled and offended. But when my wife and I realized she was going through developmental changes, we were able to say things like, "I know it is hard for you right now, but that was harsh." This softened her a bit, and when she would later join us to "hang out," her presence signaled to us that she felt safe and understood.

So many parenting techniques get labeled "game changer." But such an expression cheapens what is in fact a lifelong journey, not a game. If we can truly and profoundly absorb and understand the fact that children are most often disoriented rather than willfully disobedient, we can stand on more insightful, compassionate ground and interact with them from our best selves.

A BEING AT YOUR BEST TOOL
Be Inquisitive Rather Than Accusative

Years ago, when I first arrived in New York City, I'd hear people greet each other with the expressions like "What's up?" Or, to be more accurate, "Wazzup?" The response would range from a "Nutin' much" to a "Juz chillin'" or "Workin' hard." I was struck by how friendly and inquisitive such a simple greeting could be.

When our children are disoriented, we should create a brief pause by inwardly asking ourselves questions like "I wonder why you said that?" "What's up? Why are you so upset?" and "Am I missing something here?" A heartbeat or two can be enough to shift the trajectory of your response from reactive annoyance and mounting anger to curiosity about what might be happening to make your kid do what she did. The saying "Don't just stand there, *do something*" does not apply here. When you pause and contemplate your disoriented child's situation—however briefly—before for you act, your response will be much more healthy and well regulated. My advice: don't just do something, *be there*.

A BEING AT YOUR BEST TOOL
It's Not about Magical Answers

What I love about this approach is its simplicity. When you pause to ask the kinds of questions I outlined above, *no answer is needed*. Just the fact that you reached out to your distressed child with a question in your heart can be enough to displace and even dissolve any judgment and antipathy that might have been developing inside you. That is what matters, not a passing moment of parental brilliance (although this too is allowed).

A BEING AT YOUR BEST TOOL
Softening Can Shift Everything

Our ability to read body language has evolved over thousands of years, and children are especially good at it because their speech is still developing and they rely more heavily on the subtle signals conveyed by our postures and facial expressions. In chapter 2 we talked about identifying moments when you are clenching your body in a confrontation. If you unclench and reach out to a defiant or distraught child with genuine inquisitive concern, your eyes soften and your posture rounds off. This in turn causes them to unclench, and a tense situation can begin to diffuse.

A BEING AT YOUR BEST TOOL
Your Child or Teen Will Notice

When children and teens are their most angry selves, they are also at their most vulnerable. In such moments they are hypersensitive to any shift in the emotional current flowing between them and their parents. If we harden our facial expression, narrow our eyes, drop our forehead, or draw ourselves up, growing perceptibly larger, harder, and sharper, our children will retreat more deeply into *fight, flight, freeze,* or *flock survival modes.* However, if they pick up on an almost imperceptible softening of the eyes, relaxing of the shoulders, or unclenching of the hands, their nervous system can *stand down.* When I am able to do this with my own kids, I feel like an ancient, deeply rooted oak tree under which they can shade themselves from the withering heat of their intense emotions.

Acknowledging and understanding that our children are disoriented rather than disobedient when they act out helps us embrace a more accepting attitude. Our response can then tilt toward kindness and understanding at the very moment when our child needs our acceptance the most.

6

Derailments in the Present

WHAT PUSHES OUR BUTTONS,
AND WHAT CAN WE DO?

Over the past two decades I have given workshops exploring
the principles outlined in this book in countless communities
around the world. When we examine what pushes our buttons
in daily life, a handful of patterns emerge, no matter which culture I visit. Let's take a look at these now.

Unseen and Undervalued

We do so much for our children and teens. Sometimes we even
amaze ourselves at how good we get at pulling off a three-ring
circus day after day. During one workshop exercise, a mother of
three wrote, "Once I have pulled off all the logistical gymnastics

to pick up my kids, get them where they need to go, circle back around to pick them up, *and* get them safely home, I feel like I should be standing on a dais as everyone applauds and I receive my gold medal. Instead, my kids just trudge from the car to the door, complaining that they are hungry. All I can do is let out one of those silent screams." We all laughed as we winced in recognition.

However, when we do all that we do for our kids, we run the risk of creating and normalizing outsized expectations rather than instilling gratefulness and appreciation for our efforts and care. The result? A slow, steady bitterness builds up in us. As one workshop dad commented, "I used to do everything that was expected of me out of love, but now I often catch myself feeling resentful."

Being taken for granted, when experienced in small, daily doses, can build up a toxic charge within us. We then act out in ways that we know, in our hearts and minds, are not helpful to us as parents or to family life in general. We might burst out in anger, or we suppress a growing resentment that eventually surfaces as sarcasm, manifested in our tone of voice, facial expression, word choice, or body language. Either way, such behavior is infectious, and when our kids pick it up from us, they learn to communicate in a cynical and hurtful way.

A BEING AT YOUR BEST TOOL
Give and Ask for Small Gratitudes

Model gratitude by expressing appreciation for all the little things you, your partner, your friends, and your children do for one another. No need to exaggerate. Just make your thankfulness known in a normal tone of voice and try to make it a healthy habit.

From time to time children need to be reminded to notice and appreciate what you do for them. One couple told me they made a pact to model small gratitudes for their kids. When they are passengers in a car, for example, they make sure to thank the driver for taking them to their destination and remind their children to do the same before they get out.

It's okay to ask your child or teen for a simple *thank you* for the washed and folded clothes that magically appear on their beds. It's best to be matter-of-fact when you do this. Avoid assuming a posture of suppressed impatience, annoyance, or (particularly) long-suffering saintliness. Gently insist that your child or teen thank you for what you do for them. You may have to coach them at first by pointing out what you have done, but over time, they will catch on.

Parenting is all about paying attention to the small stuff— the myriad daily exchanges we engage in with others. When we teach our kids to express their gratitude—to say "thank you" for what has been done for them—we are doing everyone a big favor.

When It All Gets to Be Too Much

When parents speak to me about the inordinate pressures of parenting, they identify two main spheres of overwhelm. The first is family specific. With all the demands they struggle to meet just to get through a single day, parents often feel like a hapless cross between a beleaguered personal assistant and an unpaid taxi driver. And if they have two or more children, their lives can quickly devolve into tragicomedy.

The second sphere of overwhelm involves pressures that originate outside of the family. Whether it's the stress of their continuing education pursuits, mandated career retraining, or—as is most often the case—mounting pressures to meet the ever-expanding demands of daily work life, everyone agrees that the bombardment is constant.

Work pressures have certainly intensified as the use of hand-held devices has become widespread. They follow us home in our pockets or purses and alert us indiscriminately at all hours. Parents feel obligated to be available to handle work-related issues at all times, even during those moments when they know they should be focused solely on their children's needs.

The result: we are caught in a perplexing duality as we juggle the competing demands of work and family life. We *have* to stay on top of work issues to ensure job security, because our family's financial survival depends on it! But work—the provider—is also our most persistent invader. It repeatedly storms the shores of family life. What better example of this is there than the tensions that arise between parenting partners when one parent exclaims to the other: "Would you put that phone away and help me get the kids to bed!"

A BEING AT YOUR BEST TOOL
Bringing Back Balance

Let's look at some practical ways we can both shield our children and ourselves from the stressors that overwhelm our families and, at the same time, teach our kids the value of gratitude.

The beginning point for healing the overwhelmed is to question the new normal of today's supersized and fast-paced family lifestyle. Then apply the following four approaches to *simplifying life* (which I cover in more detail in my book and website Simplicity Parenting). Over the years, parents I've worked with have found these tips easily doable, really helpful, and, most importantly, liberating.

1. The Environment
    - Reduce the number of toys, clothes, and books in your home.
    - Get rid of annoying, broken, or outgrown toys.

- Keep twenty to twenty-five in each category, but put ten to fifteen away in boxes.
- Cycle two or three items in as you take the same number away.

2. Rhythm and Predictability

- Dial back on the number of choppy, arhythmical days and become aware of how many unexpected events come up. If you know you have a crazy day ahead, let the kids know the previous evening, so there are fewer unsettling surprises. If unforeseen things do come up (and they will), pay extra attention to making the days that follow a little more predictable and quiet.
- Start to build regular rhythms into your family's day. For example, the family could start offering a simple thank-you to farmers before eating dinner each evening, or you could create a comforting nightly bath-time ritual for younger children.

Rhythm builds resiliency in children. They sense that you and the home you have created are a safe harbor to which they can return and launch out into the world again.

3. Scheduling

- Cut down on the number of playdates, after-school activities, and sports.

- Allow your child time to decompress after a busy day.
- Give your kid the gift of boredom. It provides the space in which creative play and activities can develop. Such creative play can last for hours or even days.

4. Filtering Out the Adult World

- Reduce the amount of screen time your child or teen is exposed to. This is important because too much inappropriate adult information enters our kids' lives via screens.
- Cut back on the number of adult conversations you have in your child's presence. This includes talk about scary world events, personal struggles, and open criticism of authority figures, such as your child's teacher, politicians whose actions bother you, and, most importantly, your own parenting partner.
- Try to make your comments about people and events thoughtful and child friendly.
- Before you say anything in front of a child, ask yourself four questions:
    1. "Is it true?"
    2. "Is it kind?"
    3. "Is it necessary?"
    4. "Will it help my child feel secure?"

If the answer is no to any one of these questions, try to not say anything. Discuss what's on your mind later with an adult, who may want to hear it—because your child most likely does not and should not.

The Effects of Screens

I recently attended an online webinar for marketers who specialized in selling to children. It was a little like going undercover, but I needed to know more about their tactics. I was stunned to hear parents being referred to as "purchasing friction." Yes, that is actually the term that was repeatedly used when talking about a mom or a dad. The thrust of a very well organized and strategic workshop called "New Media and Removing Purchasing Friction" was how to use screens to consciously break down family life in order to sell more products.

I am not necessarily antiscreen, but I am passionately pro-connection to the things in life that form the character of our children and help them be more balanced, caring, strong, and resilient human beings. Over the years of watching kids grow, I have seen four main connections that seem particularly valuable.

The Four Concentric Circles of Connection

1. *Connection to Nature and the Outdoors*
When you ensure that your child or teen spends time in nature, they are likely to engage in timeless creative play. They have unstructured time and space to make things, practice something they love, or lay in the bough of a tree and just "be." So many

critical life skills for the future have their foundation in giving children the gift of time in the natural world.

2. Connection to Friends and Play

A child or teen needs time to develop real friends. When they spend much of their free time online, "friending" acquaintances and following strangers on multiple social media feeds, kids are robbed of the opportunity to interact with real people, which is critical to the development of their social and emotional intelligence. Friendships can be fun *and* challenging. It takes work to maintain a healthy friendship. Online "friending" is artificial and superficial: if someone displeases your child, she can "unfriend" the person with one click. No fuss, no effort, and no social development. Overuse of screens and social networking can engender a false sense of relationship entitlement. No one wants this for his child or teen.

3. Connection to Family

Ensure that your child or teen has time to simply hang out with you and her brothers and sisters. All those daily doings and conversations give your family its identity. When we spend time together we bank "relationship credits." That way, when a relationship gets strained, we can make a "withdrawal" and keep a situation from spiraling to a bad place. Furthermore, when you avoid the ubiquitous media-generated images of dysfunctional family life, in which adults are portrayed as naïve, disconnected, self-interested, and emotionally immature, you do yourself and your children a big favor, because kids absorb what they are exposed to, especially if they see it a lot.

4. *Connection to Self*

Every parent wants her child to grow up with strong moral values. Every kid wants to be true to himself, particularly as he nears his teen years. However, screens are a powerful vehicle for marketers who are pulling in the opposite direction. They are trying to convince our kids to buy their products in order to look a certain way, to feel cool, to be popular, to fit in. Giving our sons and daughters a strong sense of what constitutes morally guided decisions versus the shiny allure of constructed, fad-driven popular culture is one of the most valuable gifts of ethical discernment we as parents can offer.

Connection Takes Time

To live into each of these vital spheres of life that form the foundations of what we need to live up to our potential takes something special: time. Remember those magical days as a child when we would lie in the grass looking at the clouds moving by or play a laughter-filled game with friends or family that seemed to go on forever? Contrast this with the reality today that for tweens, those between the ages of eight and twelve, the average screen-time exposure is nearly six hours per day; for teens, the daily average is nearly nine hours, according to a 2015 study from the family technology education nonprofit group Common Sense Media. When we do the simple math, it becomes pretty clear that the day-after-day impact on a kid's life is serious. It means that every minute she is plugging into the virtual world, she is not connecting to the real world of nature, friends, family, and self.

When a child is given the time and space she needs in order to have real connected moments occur every day, she is placing another building block in what will become the structure of her life. Screens are time bandits. Anything that erodes the time our child needs to do this *has* to be regarded with suspicion and re-quires our vigilance.

The four connections I've outlined form an enduring base camp from which a child can move out into the world, return to refresh and regroup, and then push out again—and this next time, his explorations will take him a little further than before. This pattern of launching out and returning back will repeat over the years: from a toddler's conquest of the stairs, then running back to show you what he has done; to a young child's first brave bicycle exploration of the neighborhood, then her dinner-table recounting of the stories of whom she met; to a teen's first love and heartache that he confides to a very trusted friend.

As our kids grow into adults, we know we won't always be around for them. But we can rest in the knowledge that by courageously removing the barriers to their critical connections with the natural world, friends, family, and self, we gave them what they needed to develop their own inner base camp, a foundation that goes with them wherever they are and can never be taken from them.

Have Kids Work for It

To market a talk I gave a few years back, an event planner used the title "Entitlement Monsters and the Parents Who Enable Them." Its provocative, accusatory tone surprised me. I worried parents would feel affronted and stay away. Instead I walked into a room packed with concerned, frustrated parents. Truth be told, we all want to raise our children to carry a spirit of gratitude rather than a false sense of entitlement. I told them the following story, which was sent in to us.

Carla and her two sons were driving home after school when they spotted a front-lawn yard sale. Sam, her eldest, let out a shout. He'd spied a bike the likes of which he had never seen before and begged his mom to stop the car. "Oh no," she thought, "not more nagging about bikes." The eleven-year-old had been pleading with her to buy him a mountain bike for months. All his friends had them. Why couldn't he? Carla bit her lip. She was a single mom, and money was always tight. There was no way she could afford to pay hundreds of dollars for a bicycle, whether it was mountain ready or not.

The boys jumped out of the car and ran over to inspect the treasure. "Look at how long this seat is, Mom!" Sam exclaimed. "The gears shift with this big knob. The handlebars are like a

Harley-Davidson's!" "Hey, there are two!" added Brandon, his eight-year-old brother. Sam had found a pair of 1970s dragsters, which looked as cool now as they had back then. They were a bit rusty, and a jumble of grimy cogs, cables, chrome bars, and chains lay in a nearby box. But that didn't faze Sam or Brandon. "We can totally fix them up, Mom," Sam said, in as serious and convincing a grown-up voice as he could muster. The brothers' enthusiasm was so infectious that the owner reduced the price of one bike to five dollars and threw in the second bike for free.

Carla caved. "Great, so now I have, not one, but two pieces of junk," Carla thought as her boys struggled to fit everything into the trunk of the car. On the ride home she spoke to them with conviction. "This is your project, and it is completely up to you, okay?" Sam nodded. Even Brandon seemed to get it.

As soon as they got home, the boys disappeared into their small garage and started rummaging through their newfound plunder. They spread out a big drop cloth, "just like Dad does," and began to disassemble and clean all the parts. Over the next few weeks the boys' interest in the project did not waiver. Whenever Carla went out to the garage to check on their progress, she'd often find a bunch of other neighborhood kids pitching in. Dueling stories and lots of unbridled laughter punctuated the bustling scene.

Six weeks later, Project Bike Restoration had progressed almost alarmingly well. Carla wondered how they did everything but decided not to question their ingenuity. Little did she know that Sam had walked all the way across town to the local bike store and befriended the middle-aged owner, who was pleased to see a youngster so keen on restoring a pair of classic dragsters. His twenty-something employees found Sam cool, too, and put any parts they figured he might need in a pail they nicknamed "Sam's Bucket." They even adapted some of these parts to ensure they'd fit the dragsters and drew diagrams Sam could follow to put everything together properly.

Unbeknownst to their mother, Sam and Brandon also started hanging out at the local car body shop a few blocks away. There, guys with "really great beards and *so* many wicked cool tattoos" took a shine to them. The auto-shop guys cut a deal with the two brothers. They'd help them restore the bikes on the condition that the boys let each body-shop dude take the dragsters for a spin when the job was done. The boys heartily agreed.

So the bearded restoration crew rechromed the backrests and handlebars, reupholstered the banana seats, and even painted the frames midnight blue, with flames spurting forth in all the right places. To top it all off, they mounted a black number 8 billiard ball on each gearshift.

When Carla found out what the kids had done, she was stunned. "It shocked me that Sam had been going all over town. When I asked him why he hadn't got permission, he reminded me that I had told him that this project was to be his and his alone. That's when I truly realized that boys do take things literally," she said with a wry smile.

The bikes were now finished, and every boy at school loved them. What's more, Sam could speak with authority about cable adjustments, bearings, spoke replacement, and chain tension. Soon a flood of requests to restore other kids' bikes poured in. "The only problem," Carla noted with a broad smile, "was that every night we had to wash off his bike's tires." That's because Sam insisted on bringing his dragster inside, so he could have it beside his bed each night when he fell asleep.

The benefits of this experience to Sam and his family were significant:

- Grit: He had to solve multiple problems he had never encountered before.
- Process: He experienced taking a process from beginning to end.
- Family connection: He connected with his brother, who joined him in the project, and with his mother, who supported him.
- Creative thinking: He reached out into the wider community to find the resources he needed.
- Impulse control: He learned that he couldn't have everything he wanted immediately.
- Self-motivation: No one pushed him to take on and complete this project. He motivated himself over many weeks.
- Respect: He earned the respect and admiration of his school friends.
- Value: He learned the value of material things.
- Appreciation: He became much more likely to be thankful for the things he was given in the future.

- Purpose: He received a precious gift—a sense of industry and purpose.

None of this would have occurred if Carla had given in to Sam's demands and bought him a mountain bike. Our kids need to be given the opportunity to work toward what they want, whether they become directly involved in building it or they earn the money to pay for it. Most importantly, working with our kids in this manner reduces the nagging, whining, and entitlement that we find so bothersome. When they undergo such experiences, they build and strengthen emotional muscles, which power their independence and gratitude throughout their lives.

It is so hard to feel unseen, especially by our own children who we do so much for and long to love and be loved by. It can affect us in our most tender, emotional place, our hearts. I am reminded of the Zulu greeting of *Sawubona*, which I would often hear on my visits to southern Africa. Roughly translated, this means, "I see you." The response to this lovely welcome is *Ngikhona*, or "I am here." With this in mind, it seems so very important to explore why we may feel unappreciated by our children and what can be practically done about it. It is about more than our need to be valued. It's about being more fully present with them, a position that offers us a firm ground to stand on as gatekeepers to the many outside influences that will come at them as they grow—those that are unhealthy and those that will build resilience and strength of character.

7

Derailments . . . from the Future

We all have a "Circle of Influence," which is often so much smaller than our large "Circle of Concern." Being an effective parent depends a good deal on recognizing our concerns but working within what we can influence.

For example, as a mom or dad it is natural for us to worry about the future. It is built into our parenting job description. But when our hopes for our kids cross a line, it can lead us to feel anxious and even helpless. Here are some ways we can get our arms around this issue and stay balanced and healthy.

Just about all of us are aware of the shortened version of the Serenity Prayer, written by Reinhold Niebuhr and popularized in the 1940s.

God, grant me the serenity to accept the things I
  cannot change,
Courage to change the things I can,
And the wisdom to know the difference.

This came into sharp focus for me in the 1990s, when I first read *The Seven Habits of Highly Effective People*. In this well-known book, Stephen Covey speaks about the Circle of Concern and the Circle of Influence. A Circle of Concern encompasses the wide range of apprehensions we have, such as making our rent or mortgage payments, keeping our health up, or dealing with work issues, the political climate, or the threat of war. A Circle of Influence encompasses those concerns that we can do something about; they are concerns that we have some control over. Even though it might not seem like it sometimes, we do have a lot of influence over small, daily events such as bed- and mealtimes, but we also can influence larger life decisions such as medical care and college choice. It's worth noting that *influence* does not necessarily mean full *control*, as that would lead to a whole lot more family trouble and would likely have our kids seeing us as tyrants.

Covey goes further and connects these two circles to proactive and reactive people. He defines *proactive* as "being responsible for our own lives. . . . Our behavior is a function of our decisions, not our conditions." Reactive people tend to neglect those issues that are under their control and influence. Their focus is mainly on the *concerns* they have rather than on responding to them, and as a result their Circle of Influence shrinks.

An interesting way of determining which circle someone is operating within is by listening to the language they use. Circles of Concern are full of "haves" and "hads," while Circles of Influence are full of "be's." Here are some examples.

CIRCLE OF CONCERN ORIENTED:
HAVES / HADS (REACTIVE)

If only I had a husband/wife who wasn't . . .

I need to have my child in a better school . . .

If I had respect from my mother-in-law . . .

If I could just have more time to myself . . .

CIRCLE OF INFLUENCE ORIENTED:
BE'S (PROACTIVE)

I can be more emotionally regulated when my son shouts.

I can be a better role model to my kids.

I can be more understanding when my wife needs some time for herself.

I can be more available for my kids and spend less time being distracted by my phone.

I can seek out other people who can help me better understand this issue I'm confused about.

Earlier in this chapter we looked at the best-known part of the Serenity Prayer.

> *God, grant me the serenity to accept the things I*
>   *cannot change,*
> *Courage to change the things I can,*
> *And the wisdom to know the difference.*

However, there is more to this verse that is not so well known. I was struck by the next part of the passage, which seems to relate to being proactive and working out of our Circle of Influence.

> *Living one day at a time;*
> *Enjoying one moment at a time;*
> *Accepting hardships as the pathway to peace.*

A BEING AT YOUR BEST TOOL
Be More in the Moment

What this paradigm means for us as parents is that we can be proactive and focus on issues within our Circle of Influence. While this circle might start out small, it can and will enlarge.

As the months and years go by and we keep our focus on the "be's," more and more aspects of our relationship with our family will fall naturally and beautifully within our influence.

A simple exercise you can do is to get out a pen and paper and write down your own "be's" list. Think of the things that are important to you as a mom or dad. Start each sentence with "I can be . . ." When you have finished, look at the points you have written down and choose the one that seems most doable, something you could do more of today and be reasonably sure it would be effective. This is important, because if you select an item that is too big and inwardly demanding to have control over, your effort may break down quickly and actually end up causing you to shrink what you feel you can have control over.

Keep working on that one idea for a week or longer, until those actions become a comfortable part of your newly expanded Circle of Influence. For example, you might look down your list and select "I can be more understanding and listen better when my child is upset." It may be that your son is going through some changes. Things are getting strained because it is your tendency to fire back slightly sarcastic comments, which often escalate tensions. Is it within your Circle of Influence for your child not to be going through the changes he is and pushing the boundaries of what he can get away with, as kids so often do at this stage? No. But it *is* within your Circle of Influence to do your level best to withhold small, cutting quips that have become habitual in the way you speak to your child. The more you refrain from doing this, the closer the two of you will become. If your kid genuinely goes too far and becomes rude or defiant, you will have increased your influence and subtly deepened your relationship. As a result, the boundary you put in place for your child stands a much better chance of being effective and accepted.

Just Let Them Be Okay

If we think ahead to a time when our kids will be grown and moving out of our home, perhaps going off to college, maybe traveling to adventurous (but somewhat worrying) places, we all hope that we have given them the strength and resilience to work through the challenges they will encounter. Of course we hope that they will be successful and happy, but really most of us would probably settle for them just being okay. The image of our grown son or daughter falling into bad habits and negative influences is never far away from us and tends to creep into our worries when things are not going well for them.

How do we quietly nurture this hope for our kids? What can we do today that will help our children stand on their own ground in the future? Over the past thirty years of supporting families, I have come to recognize a pattern that is clear and hopeful. It is best described by a metaphor.

True North versus Magnetic North

When a parent is willing to objectively question whether "what everybody is doing" is right for his or her child, a moral compass bearing of *true north* is set in place. This question may arise over the big, life-altering decisions, but most often it comes up around small, daily choices. The decision to allow something or not, to tune in to true north, involves pausing and "going to our gut." It is as much about instinct as it is about intellect. It's about running all the large and not-so-large decisions through a moral filter of the family values that are distinctly your own.

Magnetic north, on the other hand, does not give you a fixed moral reading. It moves around and is influenced by what popular culture and current trends are doing at the time. For example, one mother of a twelve-year-old commented, "I read a couple of interesting articles, based on solid research, telling me that screen use was not good at all for my child's brain development and attention. He already was finding it hard in school to concentrate for any length of time. I thought about strictly limiting his phone and computer time, but honestly, I would have been the only parent in his class that I know of doing that, and I kind of blocked out what I knew I should do. What is wrong with me?"

There is nothing "wrong" with this mom. Every parent knows this dilemma, and it is a tough one, because your child is very likely looking at you in a pleading and intense way as she says, "But mom, totally *everybody* is allowed." When we cave in and say yes because it is so nice to see our child happy and thanking us profusely (if briefly), we are following magnetic north and suppressing the feeling that this is not the right way to go.

The Ethical Dance

Here are the two voices that play out in many decisions we make on a daily basis.

True North	Magnetic North
"Whoa, that top is way too sexy for my eight-year-old!"	"Mmm, well, it is kinda cute, and Sophia has one."
"It's simply not okay for her to be staying up until eleven o'clock every night stressing about homework."	"I know I never had pressure anything like this in middle school. But I guess it's different now. At least she is engaged and wanting to get her homework done."
"Even if his grandmother did give him the iPad, I am going to keep it for when he is old enough."	"I told her not to get him one, but do I really want to rock the in-law boat again and face everyone's disapproval?"
"She really does not need to do a second sport this season. She already is so tired."	"Do I have the energy to fight this one? At least she is keeping busy."
"I just can't bring myself to give him a smartphone at such a young age."	"If he doesn't have access to social media, won't he be left out?"

Let's presume we can come out of this ethical dance facing our true north. What can we say to our kids that communicates our values in a simple and clear way, without judging what other kids are allowed to have and do? We have to be careful not to come across as rigid, out of touch, and sanctimonious, as that kind of attitude stands a good chance of frustrating our child—with good reason. We also have to be very conscious not to put down our kid's friend and his mom or dad, as this can provoke our child to argue back in order to defend his buddy. It can lead him to say pointedly, "Jackson's mom is *really* nice and friendly and definitely not *boring*. They have way more fun than we ever do!"

A BEING AT YOUR BEST TOOL

The way to thread the needle here is to say, "I know Jackson is allowed to . . . , but in our family we . . ." In this way we are:

1. Not judging
2. Stating our family values

The overall effect of wording things this way is that we stay quietly positive while clarifying our own family's way of being. Moreover, this type of response does not involve a big moral lecture; it stands on our own ethical ground on a day-by-day basis. It might frustrate a child, but that is a small price to pay in order for him to feel the simple strength of his family, from which he can launch safely out into the world.

"Hard Wood Grows Slowly"

My family and I live on a farm in the mountains of New England. We have a big and very old farmhouse to heat during our long, snowy, and lovely winters. We do this with two woodstoves that we keep loaded up all through the day and night. It's a family affair each summer as we cut, split, and stack our firewood to prepare for the colder months. It keeps things very real. It also brings us into close contact with our forest and the types of trees we harvest. As we section the logs, we notice the growth rings concentrically layered one around the other. We can see the different colors and forms that speak about the conditions the tree lived through as it grew. The rings tell us their silent story of good times and some harsh seasons. We often pause to marvel at the density of the ash, oak, and maple woods. They are old, solid, and heavy, a contrast to the fast-growing, light, and fragile pine and other softwoods that tend to fall and break. These softwoods produce little heat when burned.

So it was a natural conversation when my friend and fellow "farmer of light," the singer, songwriter, and poet Jewel, spoke of her time in the woods. The discussion happened when we were planning a workshop together at a festival in the Rocky Mountains and got to talking about child development. We discussed how important it is for us as parents to understand that children need to be given the space and time to *have* a childhood in order to grow up strong and resilient. She said something that struck me as a profound truth: "You know, hard wood grows slowly." I knew this from my own intimate relationship with the trees on our farm, having paused so often to marvel at their grace and strength. But it was not until Jewel said it that I connected this fact with the way we can raise our children. In her book *Never Broken*, this is how Jewel so beautifully put it:

> To this day, I calibrate my inner life to what I have observed in nature, and one of the most significant lessons it has taught me is that hard wood grows slowly. I know, not the flashiest phrase, but a profound one. I watched soft wooded trees shoot up in the spring and rot only a few years later. The harder woods became friends of mine. . . .
>
> Slow growth meant thoughtful growth. Thoughtful growth meant conscious choices. It was a ladder of thought that pulled me up over the years until I arrived at one of the mottos I try to live by: hard wood grows slowly. If I wanted to grow strong and last, and not be brittle or broken easily, I had a duty to make decisions that were not just good in the moment but good for long-term growth.

When we think about our children's future, we can remember how hardwood grows rather than be derailed by our frustration to move our family along faster. Instead of thinking of our kids' lives as enrichment opportunities, we can instead see them as a series of gently unfolding experiences that, just like an oak, will slowly form solid concentric rings. Sure, we might buy into the thought that we can give our kids the edge by getting them into more activities, higher-pressure schools, and increasingly competitive sports teams. This approach to parenting will grow emotional softwood. However, if we can dial it back and slow it down, we will not only grow more resilient children, we will also help ourselves as parents grow living hardwood in *our* core being. And our kids will sense it.

Résumé Virtues versus Eulogy Virtues

A group of parents were talking in front of a New York City private school after they had dropped off their children. "Oh, it's like you need to start building your child's résumé from the time they are in first grade," one parent lamented. The rest smiled and shook their heads knowingly. Another parent replied sardonically, "Really, don't you think that's leaving it a little late, sweetheart?" Now everyone hooted with the kind of laughter that recognized the sad truth of the joke.

We are living in a society where building lists of external achievements can seem all-important. Where we know more about how to get into a top college or construct a career than about how to develop strong inner character. The *New York Times* columnist David Brooks called these kinds of achievements "résumé virtues." The pressure to rack up résumé virtues can and does trickle down all the way into parenting. When our kids don't make the cut on a competitive sports team or their grades slip, we can worry that this is going to look bad on their transcript, leading to tension at home as we try to find out what is going on. Our conversation comes from an anxious place, and our voice has an edge of pushiness. Our teenagers in particular push right back, telling us that it is none of our business and to stay out of their lives. We retort that caring for their future *is* our business . . . and you know how the rest of this conversation goes.

But in sharp contrast to these résumé virtues, Brooks also identified a second set of values, what he calls "eulogy virtues." This may sound a bit morbid, but these are the qualities that are talked about at your funeral and long after you have passed on— whether you were courageous, stood up for what you believed in, helped the people around you be better human beings, were honest with others, were a kind and caring friend. Did you bring joy into the world? Did you love your family deeply?

Even though the concept of eulogy virtues is forward looking, it does not have a forcing and hardening feel to it. When we emphasize these kinds of deeper qualities associated with character building, the conversation with our child who is not doing so well can soften; we can become focused on what she is going through and how we can understand her.

Parenting is one of the most demanding things anyone could ever take on, and there are many pitfalls and times when we feel we are falling short of who we want to be. However, deep down inside we all know we are doing something great—greater than ourselves.

The actress Dorothy Day led a life full of challenges and chaotic, even self-destructive episodes. That all changed when her daughter was born. She wrote, "If I had written the greatest book, composed the greatest symphony, painted the most beautiful painting or carved the most exquisite figure, I could not have felt the more exalted creator than I did when they placed my child in my arms."

At the beginning of this chapter, I mentioned that it is built into us as parents to look toward our child's future, but the key is whether we are looking inward to their emotional development or outward to their status in the world. It's not always easy to keep the focus on their inner growth, but it can take so much weight off our shoulders that we can be free to enjoy all the funny and dear things that happen every day. When the frustrations come up, we can see them for the temporary moments they are rather than getting caught up in nameless and nagging worries about the future. This attitude opens a space, a possibility for us to be able to respond to our children in ways we can be quietly proud of and celebrate.

PART TWO

———

THE KEY

The Compassionate Response Practice

In this section we will prepare to experience the Compassionate Response Practice as it relates to you as a parent, teacher, or care professional. We will also look at how you can use this practice to deeply understand a child and transform your relationship with and responses to him or her. We will do this by exploring:

- The power of visualization for the "parent athlete"
- The living image of yourself both in flow—when you are at your best—and when you experience an emotional fever
- A simple guided meditation that shows you how to

integrate the emotional fever and how to celebrate and grow the kind, funny, centered you

- How to use this exercise to get inside a child's experience of emotional fever and flow, plus a look at how this shifts your response
- A special section for educators and caregivers that offers practical advice and examples of how to use the Compassionate Response Practice in school and clinical settings

8

The Fourfold You

In my teens, I was what is now called an elite youth athlete. Many aspects of this overly intense experience were not so great, but one that was very beneficial involved access to sports psychologists. These professionals taught my teammates and I how to develop mental images to optimize our performance. They did this by carefully instructing us to inwardly picture key aspects of the race or the game. We practiced this exercise repeatedly until the concept was "in the zone," as they put it, and became part of our automatic responses. Visualizing taught me how to remember plays, strategies, and techniques that were often lost in the heat of the game and when many thousands of people were shouting and (hopefully) cheering. The enjoyment that came from absorbing this visualization practice led me to remain in a creative state much more often. When I became a father, I was more than a little overwhelmed at the task I had taken on. Through this practice, I was able to use this technique when I was low on energy and struggling to get back into the right headspace.

There is a very natural way to build up a visualization that leaves us with a clear image to work with. It involves identifying four simple layers that fit together in a seamless way. In fact, the fourfold model is so smooth that it is easy to overlook one of these aspects, though if you do, you instinctively feel like something is missing. The four steps consist of becoming very aware of:

- The sensations flowing within our bodies
- Our levels of vital, energetic, or life forces
- What is moving emotionally
- Our sense of self

In this chapter we will consider each of these four dynamics in turn. Our first look will be when we are in a state of *flow* and feeling strong, and then we will go through the same four steps again, only this time we will do it when we are in the state of *emotional fever*.

Here are these layers of ourselves in detail:

In Flow . . .

Layer One: The Bodily You

As we build a visualization of a time when we are in flow with our kids, we will check in on how we experience our posture. Usually there is an easy feeling of relaxation. A lot of people describe being free of tension in the muscles, their faces feeling relaxed and eyes soft. Others mention that specific areas of habitual tightening, such as in the neck or lower back, are less problematic than usual.

Layer Two: The Energetic You

Next we will move a little deeper in our experience and notice the subtle energy flow within us. In Chinese medicine this is called *chi*. The psychoanalyst Wilhelm Reich called it *orgone*, and the philosopher and esotericist Rudolf Steiner named it the *etheric body*, *life-body*, or *formative-force body*. Inventor and researcher Semyon Kirlian developed a well-known photographic process that demonstrated the life-force flow around and within living beings such as plants, animals, and humans.

In this part of the practice we will consider the vitality we experience when we visualize ourselves in flow with our family. It's common to experience general well-being or a feeling that "I have the forces within me to meet what is being asked of me." Some people have commented they have a sense of being uplifted and a rise in their vitality. It's a lovely thing and well worth the moment it takes to picture and live into it.

Layer Three: The Relational You

The emotions that move within us when we are relating to our family are strong and often clear. When we are feeling good about how things are going with our kids, we tend to be relieved and skip to whatever is next on our long list of what we have to get done. In this part of the practice, we pause and savor the experiences of being in emotional flow, which may range in sensation from bubbly and buoyant to calm and peaceful.

Layer Four: The Essential You

Right at the core of our being is our essence. It forms our sense of self and gives us the special kind of consciousness that differentiates us from plants and animals. It could be called our "I am." Our self-esteem is a part of this fundamental essence, and it allows us to develop fine ethical or moral qualities out of which we try to act each day. It is a sense of belonging, not so much to a place but to one's self; of being comfortable not only in your skin but in your sense of who you are.

The practical experience of feeling this kind of essential flow in family life happens when we are feeling strongly anchored in what we know is good and right for our children. Our hand is on the tiller, and we are oriented and confident that the direction we are setting for our family is fair and right.

In Fever . . .

Layer One: The Bodily You

When we allow images of not doing well as a parent to rise up, it is only natural that our body may be triggered to experience tensions. These constricted trouble spots are different for each one of us, but what is common is that they are usually old acquaintances that come and almost go according to our stress levels.

There is a way in which we can make cramping muscle groups work for us. They can provide us with a body-based early warning system when we are about to lose it. If we are listening, the body will tell us sooner than our mind will that the red mists are rising and we are entering the danger zone for escalation and upset.

We can train ourselves to recognize these signals by using this part of the Compassionate Response Practice to pay attention to where our muscles tighten. The practice allows us to slow things down and become literate in reading our body's book. For example, when my own red mists rise, I tend to drop my forehead, tighten my quadriceps, and lock my knees in a brace-for-impact stance. I learned this kind of posture playing contact sports of one kind or another for many years. Even though my kids can probably spot this gesture easily, I doubt I would have consciously known I did it had I not really taken the time to notice my own patterns. This awareness has been a key to my ability to pull back from countless unattractive and potentially regrettable blowups over the years.

Layer Two: The Energetic You

Picturing yourself in a situation that is not working often brings up sensations of low energy and of being drained. One mother described it as "looking down the well and finding it is dry when everyone around you expects you to provide water." Other people have said it makes them feel lackluster and deeply fatigued.

On the other hand, some have said that they can experience it as a rigid but fiery force. It is like you are taking the firewood you need to warm your house through the winter and throwing a rash amount of it on a bonfire of anger. The fire flares up in intensity, burning anyone who gets too close, but then dies down and leaves you shivering, cold, and ashamed for doing such a thing. The feeling is similar when we exert far too many of our energetic resources on a single situation. The effort may burn through the frustrating oppositional attitude coming from a child, husband, or wife, but it leaves us exhausted and soul weary afterward. Added to that, the family member whom we subjected to this flame-throwing energy very likely has backed away, leaving us lonely, isolated, and quietly humiliated.

Bringing these experiences into awareness can prevent future flare-ups and help us to be conscious of when our energy is becoming depleted or reckless. Again we add another tone to our early warning system.

Layer Three: The Relational You

Sometimes it's hard to stay on top of the tangle of emotions that arise in any given parenting day, as they sure can happen thick and fast. When people have paused and allowed an image of when they were experiencing a day or a period of time like this, I often hear "hot" words such as *frustration, anger, resentment,* and even *rage*. "Cold" terms such as *sad, miserable,* and *defeated* often come up as well.

This is one of the hardest layers to handle because it can be so charged. However, by the time we get to the "Relational You" in the Compassionate Response Practice, a strong and warm container has been created. Also, we don't dwell on this picture but treat it in much the same way as we would the flowing version of this dynamic. We work on this part of the practice until visualization comes up, and then we keep moving.

Layer Four: The Essential You

Feeling disoriented is hard, especially when we know that if we lose the plot our kids may sense it and spin out as well. It can be associated with feeling out of sync with the world around us. It can lead us to feel our objectives are being misunderstood, and if this goes on long enough, we can even start to doubt our own motives. One father was having a hard time with his nine-year-old daughter and with getting on the same page with his wife. He wrote, "I know who I am and where I stand in my job and with friends, but when I come home I feel like I am in free fall."

Again, we will not dwell on this unsettling experience but allow it to come up to the surface so we can recognize it and not have it remain lurking in the murky deeper waters of our subconscious.

In Conclusion

Looking at our lives as having four layers is not a new concept. Rudolf Steiner called us "the fourfold human being." It's also a way of understanding our lives that for many makes instinctual sense. We all know we have a body that has vitality and emotions flowing within it. Recognizing that we have a sense of self is also a basic concept. However, we tend to have dominant relationships with one or two of these layers, which puts us at risk of overlooking the others. For example, you might focus strongly on your emotions and feel this to be mainly who you are, but you could miss the subtle energy flow within yourself and as a result may easily become overwhelmed and depleted. Another person sees that it is his sense of identity and selfhood that directs the way he relates to himself and the world but may ignore his physical body's needs and not eat so well. Some people spend countless hours in the gym building up their body's strength because that is the person they feel themselves mainly to be, but they might be struggling with emotional development. The fourfold way of seeing ourselves brings an essential balance to the health of our body, mind, and spirit. Our physical health is built on the immune system of our body, which in most instances relies on the boost it receives fighting off illness. In a similar way our emotional health and sense of self are partly based on finding ways to deal with being overwhelmed and disoriented. Seeing sickness and hard times as being essential for growth is very helpful, but first we have to become conscious of the message that discomfort and illness is sending us. This is what we are attempting by carefully exploring both the flow and the fever within each of the four aspects of ourselves.

9

The Emotional In Breath

HEALING THE FEVER

Once we have developed a picture of ourselves in flow and also in fever, we can begin to move the images in a special way. This involves embracing the struggles, frustrations, and disappointments (an *in breath*) and celebrating the successes and quiet victories (an *out breath*) that every parent experiences. Let's begin with exploring the emotional in breath. This does not necessarily imply physically drawing in air (although it is fine if it works for you to use such a rhythm in this practice), but rather drawing in the visualization you have created of yourself in a soul-fevered state.

Opening Our Heart's Arms

Accepting our own challenges and the soul fever these can create within us has a parallel in caring for a sick child. For example, one of our most basic instincts is to hold our children close if they are coming down with a virus. It pulls on our heartstrings to see them feeling unwell. We recognize their tenderness and vulnerabilities, even if at times they can trigger much frustration. When the fever hits, we don't go far away. If they are small, we sit with them in our laps, rocking and humming to them. If they are older, we may quietly lie down beside them, telling stories from our own childhood and keeping them company until they fall asleep. Our intuition is to move in close and draw them near.

What about when we come down with our own parenting soul fever? We can do precisely the same thing. We can draw our own struggle toward us, just as we would do with a fevered child, only in this case we figuratively open our heart's arms, reach out to our feelings of being overwhelmed or disoriented, and bring them in close. If we can do it for our children, why not tap into that same caring wisdom for ourselves when we are not doing so well?

Holding Away

Some years ago I was speaking with a group of moms and dads in a workshop about how tricky it becomes when we ignore our parenting problems. I used the phrase "holding away our baggage" in trying to describe the tendency we have to not look too closely at the things that are not going well. After all, these emotions are uncomfortable, so it is only natural to not want to dwell on those feelings. My briefcase was beside me, and it seemed like a good metaphor. It was "baggage" in a real way. I picked it up and held it at arm's length away from me. While it didn't feel heavy at first, the longer I held it in this way, the heavier it seemed to get. I continued to speak in what I hoped was a coherent way, but my arm was starting to shake with the stress of holding the bag. I realized that although I could appear somewhat normal, my attention was split between the heaviness of the bag and my attempt to keep communicating. The longer it went on, the more difficult it got, and finally I had to stop. I had only two choices: drop the bag or bring it in closer to my body. When I put the briefcase up against my chest, it was such a relief. The weight was suddenly much less. I could now think clearly. The folks at the workshop laughed in recognition at how close this example was to what we tend to do with our problems and how holding them at arm's length can cause them to weigh on us.

As we know, if we put a difficulty out of mind and beyond reach, it won't simply and conveniently go away. Life doesn't work like that. In time, the problem will develop a life of its own and become a part of who we are. However, the law of emotional optics comes into play here: what we look away from in an attempt to not see—what we don't like about ourselves—will be highly visible to others. Why? Because these are emotional blind spots. And although people might still like us, they may well experience something that is hard to put their finger on but nevertheless feels a little off.

But Won't It Hurt?

Some people are intuitively open to embracing the rough times we face as parents and the feelings of self-doubt and defeat that can arise; however, most of us experience this as challenging. In particular, the rest of this chapter is for those of us who need to look at this principle from a few more angles to see if we are comfortable with it.

It's normal to feel apprehensive about embracing a problem and emotionally drawing it toward us. To explore this concern is important. There was an attention-grabbing headline in the *New York Times* on August 10, 2012: "Beware the Nocebo Effect." The term *nocebo effect* grew out of the well-known placebo effect, which researchers use in many clinical trials to determine the effectiveness of new treatments by giving the real medication to only one of two groups and giving the other group an inert preparation that the subjects are told is the real thing.

Two examples of the nocebo effect occurred in studies where patients received a salt solution and were informed it was a chemotherapy drug; some 30 percent lost their hair, and 80 percent vomited. In an even more dramatic example, a participant in an antidepressant drug trial was given placebo tablets—and then swallowed twenty-six of them in a suicide attempt. Even though the tablets were harmless, the participant's blood pressure dropped perilously low. I bring this up not to pass judgment on very real health struggles any person can have, but to highlight the strength of the mind-body experience.

In Shakespeare's play *The Winter's Tale*, the strength of the mind-body relationship is the central theme. The king utterly believes his queen is being unfaithful, and he even doubts that their children are his own. His long-trusted courtiers and advisors keep telling him his belief is wrong, that the queen is true to him, but he obsessively seeks out tiny situations that he twists and exaggerates to convince himself that he is correct. In doing so, he misses many little signs of his wife's loyal love and the true words of his friends and advisors. The result is of course tragic. Ultimately the king in his turmoil imprisons his wife and puts her on trial. Even after consulting the Oracle (a long-trusted voice speaking to him directly from the spirit world), which tells him that she is true and the children are his, he continues to believe his own delusions. In a classic moment of Shakespearian convergence, the king absolutely denies the truth the Oracle speaks, and his wife goes into a deep coma upon hearing news that her son is dead, leading to the king's ultimate crisis. In the deepest tragic moment, the frozen winter of his soul breaks open, and the new life of spring begins. His repentance takes him on a spiritual journey for the next sixteen years. He learns to care about the people around him, listening to the stories of their lives and how they see the world. At the dramatic end of the play, he is reunited with his wife, whom he had thought was dead.

Phew, a happy ending! But the power of the story lies in how a belief can take on a life of its own.

Making Conscious Choices

The unsettling truth of the emotions that arise from our negative experiences is that they are coming toward us anyway. The choices we have are to be conscious or to be blindsided. To know that hard feelings exist but to look away and insist on being cheerful is a risky option to choose.

We might have reservations about bringing our baggage in close. I have heard some people comment that they don't know if they really should let these difficult feelings in. However, these feelings are in us already, and the question is much more about what we do about them. My friend Jaimen McMillan, founder of the Spacial Dynamics Institute, says wisely, "We can't control what comes at us in life, but we can decide where and how we meet it."

Bad News Becomes Good News

So many apps now allow us—no, beg us—to review the experience we just had at a restaurant or store. This subjective review culture seems to have spilled over into other aspects of our lives, and the tendency we have as parents to judge ourselves harshly probably has not been immune to it. For example, I remember a bizarre situation when I set the GPS to find our way to a place in a forest that had a famous ancient redwood tree. My family and I sat quietly before the magnificent tree, awed by its presence for quite some time. With a new sense of wonder toward the natural world, we got back on our motorcycles, ready to ride on. A screen popped up on my smartphone, asking us to review the tree and our experience! I remember thinking, "How do you put a star rating on a digital device for an experience of inner peace?" We smiled as we considered that a tree that had stood for a thousand years, had withstood countless fires and droughts, was probably not going to care too much about the score we gave it.

This experience set me thinking about our rating culture. Only a little bit of digging around the research on the topic was very revealing. Here's how is works: For every dozen or so positive reviews a restaurant receives, it takes only one or two bad ones to wipe out the good impression the reader may have. So it is clear that negativity has more influence than positivity. *But wait, there's more*, as the television ads would say when I was a kid. If the owner of the restaurant responds to the negative review openly and honestly, not only is the adverse impression erased, the response actually increases readers' positive impression of the establishment and its service.

The Compassionate Response Practice helps us do what we need to transform a bad self-review into positive self-esteem: candidly accepting and embracing that we don't always get it right without the need to justify ourselves, push back, and go into denial. Moreover, this practice can leave us with an uplifted feeling of self-worth and renewed confidence so that we can provide a well-regulated emotional safe harbor for our kids.

Being Gentle with Ourselves

The Compassionate Response Practice allows us to become much more conscious about emotions that parenting brings up, and it does it in a way that is kind. (It would be ironic to be undertaking a forceful exercise in order to be able to respond more compassionately.) A key here is that it gives equal space to both the fever and the flow within us. The practice does not overly focus on the trouble and self-doubt; it does not push through this doorway uninvited. Werner Herzog, the well-known film director, put it well when he said in an interview on National Public Radio:

> There is far too great an emphasis placed on psychotherapy and knowing all there is to know about one's self. A knowing in a greedy thinking way.
>
> If you illuminate brightly every corner of your house, night and day, continually, you will cease to have any mystery. Your house will become unlivable. It will drive you out. This is what modern psychotherapy and much of the new age movement is doing. We get fascinated by the illumined detail, but it is the wrong kind of light.

In the Compassionate Response Practice we shine a light on both our successes and our challenges. It is a soft light of self-forgiveness for our many failures to be the parent we want to be—and a quiet celebration of the times when we get it right.

The Moral Out Breath

RELEASING THE FLOW

As parents we have high ideals, and sometimes, to our surprise, we actually live up to them. We may not talk about these values much, but they are sitting just below the surface. And when we even come close to doing well, the feeling can range from quiet contentment to a joy that floods us and sometimes brings us to tears. Or it may result in a private fist-pumping happy dance done somewhere discreetly out of sight. But mainly we just feel relief to have gotten it vaguely right and conclude that maybe this parenting job we promoted ourselves into is worth it.

In this section we are going to prepare for the next step in the Compassionate Response Practice by exploring how we can grow these moments of subtle parental greatness. We will enjoy the warmth of our competence and let it flow outward, allowing ourselves to bath in its gentle radiance. In this sense it is an emotional out breath. (Again, this does not mean that you have to focus on breathing out in a physical sense during the practice itself, although it is fine if this works well for you.) The out breath is the counterbalance to the drawing inward of the image of our fevered self.

Let's dig a little deeper, allowing ourselves to recognize our own confidence and competence. In this way we grow the flow.

Permission to Brag

In our family we sometimes say, "Okay, here comes a brag" when something we have done has gone well or has been appreciated. It might be a teacher at school recognizing an essay that a lot of work was put into or a broken fence on our farm that was spotted and repaired just in time before the animals got out. I am prone to asking Katharine, my wife, and my kids, "What were the triumphs today?" Almost always there is some good and heartwarming response about a small achievement. I am not sure why the Presbyterian-inspired mantra my mother would often say, "Self-praise is no praise at all," did not stick, but I just love hearing about my family's little victories. I can't imagine not wanting to know how problems were faced and overcome and to see the smile or sparkle in their eyes as they relate what happened.

Kindling the Spark of Genius

It is often easier to celebrate others than to recognize one's self. For example, we may have a great idea, but rather than speaking it out of our own truth, we will find someone else who said it and quote him or her to prove that it is a valid idea. Feeling worthy is not easy for many, especially when it comes to being a mom or dad. The famous passage from Marianne Williamson's *A Return to Love* (a quote that is often misattributed to Nelson Mandela) seems to sum it up well:

> Our deepest fear is not that we are inadequate. Our deepest fear is that we are powerful beyond measure. It is our light, not our darkness that most frightens us. We ask ourselves, Who am I to be brilliant, gorgeous, talented, fabulous? Actually, who are you not to be? You are a child of God. Your playing small does not serve the world. There is nothing enlightened about shrinking so that other people won't feel insecure around you. We are all meant to shine, as children do. We were born to make manifest the glory of God that is within us. It's not just in some of us; it's in everyone. And as we let our own light shine, we unconsciously give other people permission to do the same. As we are liberated from our own fear, our presence automatically liberates others.

Why Hold It So Close?

We tend to hold our dearest memories and moments of brilliance close. This makes sense because they give us comfort, but the potential problem is that we can grip them too tightly, and what was formerly a lovely feeling can become a fixed image that loses its warmth and vitality. The Compassionate Response Practice reverses this tendency and asks us to release these wonderful moments and let the image of them expand and grow until it envelops us in its luminosity. To do this we use a specific image of when we were in flow with ourselves and our kids as kindling to start the fire, then move this image outward until it creates a radiating warmth that fills us with a quiet joy.

Giving Yourself Permission

If you told a friend about a situation that went well and she then asked you to say more about your part in it, you would likely feel that it was okay to speak honestly about what you did that brought about really positive results. So why not use this energy to ask, "What do I do for myself and my family that is deeply and simply good?" One mother told me of the times she had "lost it" and had used a swear word within her child's hearing. She felt ashamed, and her shame turned to despair when her son picked up the word and used it himself a couple of times.

Understandably, this triggered self-doubt. "Have I really blown it this time?" she thought. I asked her how many times she had spoken with care and kindness to her child. "Oh, I don't know, a lot," she replied. "No, really, let's figure it out," I responded. She was a stay-at-home mom with a young child, so there was a lot of contact between them. We first estimated the number of reassuring comments she was liable to make in an hour. Then we did the simple math and found that over a period of a month she was very likely to have made around five hundred loving comments!

You can probably see where this conversation went. When I asked her how many times a month she used harsh words or let a swear word slip out, it was less than twenty times. We might not all be sports fans, but a game where the score was five hundred versus twenty would, in anyone's reckoning, be counted as a major win. Large tears welled up in her eyes as she quietly said, "Yeah, thank you. I guess I need to remember that."

Golden Moment Journal

Many of us have kept journals or diaries for short or long periods of time. They tend to be a free and safe space, a place for us to honestly reflect on how our lives are going and what is moving inside us.

A Golden Moment Journal is an integral tool for preparing to do the Compassionate Response Practice. It is a little different from a regular journal, because it gives you the chance to focus on just one specific area of your life: your parenting successes. Here's how it works. Each night, take a few minutes to remember back through the day and find a moment or two when you experienced the kind of flow we explored in chapter 8. Look for moments when you were able to relax, when your energy levels were good, when you felt calm and centered. If you are especially lucky, you might identify two or three times when things were going well, but that's not the main point. What's important is to delve into how the experience felt. Savor it, bathe in it, and let yourself fully enjoy this small miracle of parenting competence.

There is seldom a day when some tiny piece of goodness does not happen. It's not that those moments don't exist, but rather that we tend to set our standards unreasonably high or else we are so tired at the end of the day that taking even thirty seconds to reflect seems hard. One couple said that they would recall their golden moment of the day together just before turning off the light to go to sleep. Usually at least one of them remembered something, and, even better, it helped them end the day on an upswing and to "go to sleep smiling," as the father said.

Many people have commented that this practice is good to do in the evening, as it counterbalances the worries and anxieties about family that tend to come up at night. A young dad was trying to overcome doubts about not being settled and mature enough to help raise his baby daughter. He decided to write down in a journal, once a day, what he called his "moments of minor brilliance." He would do this every evening before going to sleep. He shared with me a reflection from the part of his journal he kept for "random thoughts." He wrote: "Late at night. I am so tired. Here come all my doubts. They seem to creep in. Lie in bed lost in thoughts of hopelessness." A few weeks later: "When I began to do this [the journal], the bad feelings did not exactly go away but now they don't overwhelm me anymore." After a couple of months, he observed: "The moments of minor brilliance are getting bigger. Wow, I think I am actually beginning to know when I am living one in real time not just remembering it after the fact. This is great. Maybe it's become kind of a habit? Funny how I didn't see that coming. Like it."

Another father who owned a small but high-pressure construction business talked about how this practice helped him. "I used to lay in bed worrying about my business and whether I was going to make it all work. I had grown up not having much security, and I especially stressed over paying the mortgage and keeping my kids provided for. So rather than count sheep, I began to count my blessings and golden moments of the day with my kids and wife. It kind of forced me to look at the things that really mattered and how we were doing okay. It gave the perspective I needed, and the nervousness I was feeling seemed to settle down."

A grandmother who was raising her granddaughter made an interesting comment about time. She said, "The day went by so fast that I felt a sense of achievement if I just got through all I had to do. Keeping this journal revealed something quite unexpected. I found that after a week or two I began to notice the golden moments when they were happening, and to my surprise it was like the day seemed to slow down and not be so rushed." When asked why she thought that might have happened, she replied, "Perhaps it was because it gave me a chance to take a breath and be in the present rather than trying to move my granddaughter on all the time."

The Golden Moment Journal can be a special blank book you find in some lovely store, or it can be a regular old exercise book. Some people have used their phones to record their own voices and replay their words at times in the day when they needed reassurance. What matters most is that you take the time to reflect on that beautiful experience of flow. Maybe it was a drop, a trickle, or even a gush—the core feeling is the same, and it can give us a lift when we need to know that we are capable of moments of quiet brilliance.

A New Trajectory

One aspect of the Compassionate Response Practice is based on embracing negative emotions and images of one's self and others. It gives us a way to accept charged emotions and the difficult aspects of a relationship that have become fixed and rigid. It also helps us to not fall into a pattern of fear-based self-fulfilling prophecy and casts an honest yet caring light on our emotional reactions.

Emotional Photosynthesis

There is a vital balance we need to strike between facing our challenges and embracing our successes. As we have explored, the point is not to push away or deny the aspects of ourselves that are not yet working as we would hope, but also not to ignore that we often get it right.

There are good parallels between the way plants process toxins in the atmosphere to produce the clean air we need and the ways we can work with our soul fevers and flows to be a better parent. It's interesting that plants actually need carbon dioxide's interaction with light and water to generate oxygen. Similarly, we need to absorb what can feel very challenging, even noxious, about the way we relate to our kids and allow this to come into an emotional chemical reaction with the flowing, light-filled aspects of our parenting. The result is a good, clean, health-giving atmosphere that the whole family can take in and be nourished by.

11

The Compassionate Response Practice

PHASE ONE

By now, I hope you have a good idea of what this practice is about and the transformation it can help you achieve. In this chapter you will be guided through the first of the two phases of the practice itself. This phase will focus on carefully building up an image of times in your life when you were in flow with your family and also bring in the visualization of when things were not going well.

Initially you will need to read the instruction, put the book down, and work on the element described. The sections have been carefully designed to be self-contained and easy to remember and follow. In time, the written guidance will serve less as an instruction and more as a reminder, and after a handful of times you will be able to put the book away and glance at it only when needed. Just like when you're learning lines for a play, at first the experience is slow and you need to keep checking the script. But because this practice is so much about your individual human experience, the time it takes from first learning the process to feeling that "yes, I've got this now" is quite short. After a week or two, the practice will take you less than a couple of minutes to do. However, when you are in the learning phase, you will need about ten to fifteen minutes.

Step One: Time and Place

Even though this practice is not going to take a lot of time, it is great if you can find a relatively quiet place to do it. Over the years I have heard some funny stories about how parents have found places to be alone to practice—everything from the car (the mobile dojo) to the bathroom, although the latter is not a guaranteed place of solitude if you have young children. Many people find a short walk in nature or around the park will do it. Sometimes you might need to share your intention with a partner or a friend and ask them to watch the kids for fifteen minutes.

Working parents have said that when they do it at lunch or break time during the workday, it helps them feel much more centered and less anxious for the rest of the day. A father told a workshop group that he would practice it as he was tidying up his desk at the end of the day. "Because I did this," he explained, "when I got home I was more prepared for entering back into things and did not transfer my work frustration onto my kids." As we covered previously, probably the most common time people pick is during their nighttime routine. One parent figured out that his focus was helped if he sat on the bed rather than lying down. A mother commented, "If I fall asleep doing it, at least I am going to sleep happy." Another dad's words came right from the practical wisdom of parenting when he wryly said, "I loudly announce that it is chore time, and miraculously I find myself alone."

Step Two: Inwardly Preparing

Having a small ritual can be helpful in setting a mood. This is particularly useful when you are first learning the practice. The most common routine is to play a favorite soothing piece of music or say a special verse, passage, or poem right before embarking on the first visualization. Others use a meaningful painting or card that they take a moment to look at again. Some people like to focus their minds by observing a plant, a tree, or a favorite landscape for a moment or two, noticing any changes the season or time of day might be producing.

At the back of this book I have included some examples of verses and poems that have been shared with me over the years. The Bible and Rumi's poetry are the most often used, but of course there exist many inspirational verses. Sometimes you might just lift one or two meaningful lines from a passage rather than trying to remember the whole thing. For years I have used a verse of Adam Bittleston called the "Intercessory Prayer," which I adapted so that it focuses on one's own inner process. I also love his verse "Against Fear," which is also included.

So before you go any further, select a verse or poem from the appendix or pull out something you might already have. If you are using a passage in written form, say it slowly and quietly to yourself now. If you are using an inspiring image, turn to it now and take a few moments to absorb the meaning it has for you.

Step Three: Flow

Think of a particular moment, a special day, or a period of time when you were at your best with your family, something that stands out when you look back. Create a living inner picture of yourself in that state of parenting flow.

Take your time, breathe deeply, and let this image arise. When you are ready, move on to exploring it more deeply through the following sequence.

Your Body
Let the warmth of your experience fill your body. In this golden time you may see and experience . . .

Relaxed face muscles

Soft eyes, shoulders, chest

Restful arms

Gentle hands

Warmth of the image flowing down through your pelvis
and thighs, in and around your knees

Feet spread like large, soft lion's paws

"I am in deep ease."

Your Energy

In this golden time you may see and experience that . . .

Vitality is streaming

My inner vigor and capacity can easily meet the demands
of life

Life forces grow within me

"I am resilient."

Your Feelings

In this golden time you may see and experience yourself as . . .

Buoyant

Calm

Fun loving

Accepting

"I am balanced."

Your Sense of Self

In this golden time you may see and experience that you are . . .

Open to the future streaming toward me

In sync

Trusting and trusted

Decisive

Authoritative

"I am centered."

Now begin to soft-focus on the image you have built. Then put it to one side and create space for a new visualization to arise.

Step Four: Fever

Think of a particular moment, a specific day, or a period of time when you were really struggling, something that stands out when you look back. Create a living inner picture of yourself in this parenting fever, when things were hard and not going well with your family.

Take your time, breathe deeply, and let this image arise. When you are ready, move on to exploring it more deeply through the following sequence.

Your Body

In this fevered time you may see and experience . . .

Tension in your face muscles

Eyes narrowing

Shoulders and chest hardening

Arms tightening

Hands clenching

Legs locking

Toes gripping and contracting

"I am constricted."

Your Energy

In this fevered time you may see and experience that . . .

My vitality is low

I feel wilted and lethargic

I am stiff

My energy is jagged

I feel cramped

My inner forces are being flooded by the demands of life

Life forces drain away

"I am overwhelmed."

Your Feelings

In this fevered time you may see and experience feelings of . . .

Heavyheartedness

Frustration, anger

Agitation

Humorlessness

Blame

"I am raw."

Your Sense of Self

In this fevered time you may see and experience feeling . . .

Anxious about the future

Out of sync with your family

Worried and mistrustful

Unsure and indecisive

Little objectivity

Taking things very personally

Rigid, stiff, and authoritarian

"I am disoriented."

Step Five: The Whole You

As we did previously, soft-focus on the picture you have built and then put it slightly to one side so that you can see the two visualizations, you in the flow and in the fever, standing next to each other. Try to balance the two images so that neither dominates. In your mind's eye, look from one to the other: light and dark, levity and gravity, flow and fever.

This is the whole you. Your struggles and sadnesses are as

real and necessary as your successes. Take your time and, as best you can, look at them both with equanimity.

Well done. You have completed the first of the two phases of the Compassionate Response Practice. In the next chapter we will begin to move these images so that we integrate the fever and release the flow. The second phase is, for many, a beautiful and liberating experience.

12

The Compassionate Response Practice

PHASE TWO

Using Moral Breathing

Many paths of self-development involve the conscious use of breath. In this phase of the Compassionate Response Practice, we will use the gesture of breathing but in a different way, a way that I call "Moral Breathing." As we have discussed in previous chapters, rather than focusing on the physical act of breathing in, you will take the visualization related to emotional fever and draw it toward you, moving it inward and integrating it. Then you will release in an outward direction the image of yourself in flow. If this expansion and contraction happen to coincide with the natural rhythms of your breathing, it's perfectly fine, but try not to limit yourself to having the pictures you are working with comply with your physical breathing.

In this part of our practice you will see the term "heart's arms." It is used for release of our golden higher being and also for reaching out to our fevered self. We have many terms that are similar, such as "our hearts leapt," "heavyhearted," and "heart's warmth," to name a few. This particular use of the phrase is not meant to relate only to our physical heart but to denote an expressive gesture of our deeper self. It is a gentle but powerful image that frees our feeling life from being a passive receiver of impressions and makes it possible to use it as an active helper of our intent.

You will also see the term "sea of compassion." This is a place in ourselves that we come to know primarily when a life-altering event occurs within our family or to our friends and sometimes in response to a tragic world event. However, this vast, limitless, and deep space lives within us at all times. In this practice we open up pathways to this capacity without waiting for life's big occurrences to take us there. We then use it to cultivate compassion for ourselves, as this is what brings about one of the most important and elusive shifts every parent needs: to forgive ourselves for all the many times we have not lived up to our own parenting ideals. After all, how can we be at our best unless we accept and pardon ourselves for the times we have been at our worst?

Step One: Radiate

- Return your focus to the whole you. See both images, you in flow and you in fever, side by side.
- Open your heart's arms and welcome the flowing image you have created.
- Hold it close, but hold it lightly.
- Feel the cumulative warmth of your ease, resiliency, balance, and centeredness fill your chest.
- Take your time and allow the loving abundance you feel for your family to permeate you. Allow it to flow upward through your neck and head and downward through your lower body. As it does this, it grows not only in warmth but also in light.
- Embrace this light in your heart's arms and reach outward.
- Share it. Let it go, grow, and glow. Let it gently radiate all around you.
- Feel the calm, steady, and centering warmth you have created.

Step Two: Integrate

- With your heart's arms extended, reach out to the emotional-fever image.
- Just as you would a fevered child, hold your struggling

self with love, cradle it, and draw it toward you, but only as close as is comfortable.

- Look down on your fevered self with the same care you would a fevered child and see it with interest and quietness.
- The nearer it comes, the more the weight of emotions you have held for so long lightens.
- As you draw it closer, place it as a single drop in the vast sea of compassion you have within yourself.
- Quietly and slowly say to yourself, "I forgive me."
- What was heavy is now light.
- What was restless is now still.
- What was disorienting is now centered.

Step Three: Radiate and Integrate

Repeat the above process at least two or three more times. With your heart's arms, first release and radiate the loving and centered image of yourself in flow. Then draw the struggling, fevered self toward you and envelop it in your compassionate self-forgiveness.

Step Four: Unify

Now move the fevered image inward, just as you have been doing, but this time release the flowing image outward at the same time. If you can, allow the two to meet and merge. Don't worry if this does not happen at first. It's not easy. Take your time.

No longer separated . . .

> *Dark melds with light,*
> *Chaos melds with calm,*
> *Gravity melds with levity,*
> *Fever melds with flow.*

This is the unified you.

> *I am me*
> *I am one*
> *I am*

Step Five: Closing

Maintain your quiet just a little longer. Let the experience of unity you have created have the space it needs to be fully absorbed. If you feel words arise inside, listen to them and write them down when you are ready. Here is an example that came up for a father who was struggling to break out of angry reactions: "It is strong to be kind and kind to be strong." A small verse or motto of this sort can be something you return to whenever you are triggered by a challenging situation with your child.

Likewise, if an image arises, give it space. Many years ago, a vivid picture arose for me at this last stage of the practice. It was of a sturdy, mature, and very deeply rooted oak tree. It was summer, and the dense leaves on the spreading boughs gave a cooling shade from the hot sun above. As I was considering the image, I noticed there was a rope swing on which my children were playing. It made me smile. After that, whenever I would feel the red mists of frustration rising, I would often recall this image, and it created a lovely space for me to quietly accept my overheated and my cool self. It helped me remember I was the shade my children could find shelter under.

These images and words are not ordinary. They come from a much deeper place. Some people have said that they feel they are "heaven sent" or "soul food"; others have simply commented that they are a "God-given gift." I like that one.

The practice is now yours. The following chapters will focus on what happens when you use it right in the moments when in the past you would have been likely to fall into the old, unwanted, action-reaction patterns with your kids. And that is the real point of this exercise. It is something that is so pleasing—no, actually, it is thrilling.

13

The Compassionate Response
for a Child in Need

"Can I do this same exercise but focus on a child or teen, rather than myself?"

To anyone who has been using the Compassionate Response Practice for even a short time, it quickly becomes clear that this can be applied to many other relationships. Of course, the first thought that comes up for parents is to shift the focus from their own challenges to the struggles of their children. Caregivers and teachers also come to the same thought regarding the children and teens they serve.

In essence, we use the same process. Rather than concentrating on yourself, you create a visualization of a child, first in flow and then in fever. After doing this, you use the Moral Breathing technique we learned in chapter 12 to draw toward you and integrate the image of the emotionally fevered child, then to expand and rejoice in the light-filled image of the same child in flow. This process addresses the whole child and is a good way of thinking about children in general. It specifically helps us break out of the increasing tendency to pathologize, to overfocus on behavioral symptoms, or to coldly analyze children. It opens a way to *name and know* the child's struggles rather than *label and limit* the child for life.

This whole-child practice offers three benefits:

1. Support and understanding of the child. When we take the time to live into the child's experience, we are much more likely to be accurate and empathetic. This also helps us avoid judgments and false presumptions that can cause frustration and further escalation.

2. Self-regulation. It is often the same child in your family or classroom who triggers you over and over. Focusing this practice on a child opens the possibility of breaking out of old, negative action-reaction cycles as your response to the challenging behavior becomes centered and genuinely calm.

3. Integration. It is hard not to become drawn into the challenging behavior of a child. Over time this can build up antipathy, cloud perspectives, and lead to a

relationship habit that is difficult and even destructive for everyone involved. The young person feels, "She just hates me," and the adult sees a "problem child." What this practice offers is both a way to widen the aperture of your perspective and a strategy that allows you to understand the child's struggles while recognizing the beautiful child he is.

Certainly for a parent and also for an educator, caring for a child who feels unwell and has a physical fever is natural. If she is young we hold her close, perhaps hum a little song or just sit quietly with her, letting her know by our presence that she is safe. Maybe it's because of this instinct that doing the same thing for an emotionally fevered child seems intuitive. In one situation we hold a child with our physical arms, and with another we do just the same thing with our invisible but strong heart's arms.

In this version of the practice you will be asked to reach out, gather up a struggling child, and inwardly hold him close. However, you may need a little practice at this before it feels as natural as caring for a sick child. It could feel challenging to allow this kind of emotional proximity, particularly if you have built up strong antipathies. You may have developed an unconscious gesture of holding the problem at arm's length, which is understandable if in the past you had few strategies for transforming your frustration. The fact that you have chosen this child to support might mean that on a deeper level you are ready to bring the baggage of your animosity closer and, by doing so, lighten the burden of the relationship. However, if any reticence comes up for you in the in breath stage of this exercise, be gentle with yourself and draw the image of the fevered child toward you only as close as feels comfortable. In time you almost certainly will be able to increase the nearness of the image and your welcoming gesture to it, but for now do what feels right and no more.

How to Use This Chapter

In this chapter you will find a description of the now familiar fourfold picture of the flow and fever states. The Moral Breathing you experienced earlier when you were working on this practice for your own needs will follow the same pattern, but it will be framed with a child in mind. Rather than ask you to translate the adult-oriented guidance given earlier, I have reworked and slightly reworded the steps so that you can seamlessly move into focusing on a child. I hope the use of the same framework and similar wording will not seem repetitious but rather serve as a review and a supportive reminder. Some paragraphs will be reproduced with only minor changes so that you don't have to flip back and forth between chapters. I've made some changes you will not want to miss in the text and added a few completely new stories and points of guidance.

This chapter also takes into account that some people may prefer to start with a whole-child-oriented version of the Compassionate Response Practice rather than the practice focused on the adult, and as such they will need this information laid out here in full. My hope is that even if you already read about some of these concepts in the earlier chapters, you will benefit from reading them again in the context of working with a child in need and may gain a different and deeper perspective.

Step One: Time and Place

As before, find somewhere that you will be able to have an undisturbed ten to fifteen minutes alone. Sometimes that's asking a lot, and if it is not possible, it shouldn't deter you. A car journey, gardening, or a walk to the bus stop works well for this kind of exercise and can be used as meditative time.

Step Two: Inwardly Preparing
Selecting the Child to Carry

The next step in this preparation is to choose the child you are going to hold through the meditation. For a parent it can be an easy choice, but an educator may need to give it some thought. The obvious choice is a child who can trigger you. This choice will often involve your wish to transform the antipathies that can arise. However, you may decide to take a quiet child who is often overlooked, as he does not draw attention to himself with rowdy behavior or social controversy. Alternately, it could simply be a child who is a mystery to you and whom you wish to better understand so you can help her.

The Token and Ritual

I like to put some token representing the child in front of me. It can be a painting or craft project the child created at home or in school. It might take the form of a special photograph in which the soul of the child seems to shine through. Simple things like a bowl of unusually colored shells or pebbles the child collected on a lovely holiday can be put nearby. Take a moment to gaze at the token to renew your sense of this wonderful being. After this, you might like to say a special verse or poem that is meaningful to you in this context (see the appendix for some suggestions). I like to turn to Adam Bittleston's "Intercessory Prayer," as I particularly value these words. They don't speak generally about my good wishes but rather are directed to the child's guardian being, asking that the hopes expressed be given to the child through this spiritual channel.

Step Three: Flow

Think of a particular moment—a special day or a period of time when the child was at his or her best, something that stands out when you look back at your time with this child. Create a living inner picture of the child in flow. (Note: In the description that follows I will use the word *child* for expediency's sake. However, this does not mean that this practice cannot be used when supporting a teenager.)

Take your time, breathe deeply, and let this image arise. When you are ready, move on to exploring it more deeply through the following sequence.

The Physical Body of the Child

In this golden time create a living picture of the child with . . .

> Relaxed face muscles
> Soft eyes, shoulders, chest
> Restful arms
> Gentle hands
> "The child is in deep ease."

The Energy Flow of the Child

In this golden time create a living picture of the child whose . . .

> Vitality is streaming
> Inner vigor and capacities can easily meet the demands
>   of life
> Life forces are growing and thriving
> "The child is resilient."

The Emotional Current

In this golden time create a living picture of the child feeling . . .

Buoyant

Calm

Fun loving

Accepting

"The child is balanced."

The Child's Sense of Self

In this golden time create a living picture of the child being . . .

Open to the future streaming toward him or her

In sync

Trusting and trusted

Decisive

Clear

"The child is centered."

Now begin to soft-focus on the image you have built. Then put it to one side and create space for a new visualization to arise.

Step Four: Fever

Think of a particular moment—a specific day or a period of time when this child was really struggling—something that stands out when you look back. Create a living inner picture of the child in this emotional fever, when things were hard and not going at all well for him or her.

Take your time, breathe deeply, and let this image arise. When you a ready, move on to exploring it more deeply through the following sequence.

The Child's Body
In this fevered time create a living picture of the child with . . .

> Face muscles tensing
>
> Eyes narrowing
>
> Shoulders and chest hardening
>
> Arms tightening
>
> Hands clenching
>
> Legs locking
>
> Toes gripping and contracting
>
> "The child is constricted."

The Child's Energy
In this fevered time create a living picture of the child . . .

> Whose vitality is low
>
> Who feels wilted and lethargic
>
> Who is stiff
>
> Whose energy is jagged
>
> Who feels cramped
>
> Whose inner forces are being flooded by the demands
>   of life

Whose life forces drain away
"The child is overwhelmed."

The Child's Feelings

In this fevered time create a living picture of the child experiencing emotional currents that are . . .

Sharp and pointed

Heavyhearted

Frustrated, angry

Agitated

Humorless

Blaming

"The child is emotionally raw."

The Child's Sense of Self

In this fevered time create a living picture of the child feeling . . .

Anxious about the future

Out of sync with family or classmates

Worried and mistrustful

Unsure and indecisive

Little objectivity

Taking things very personally

Rigid, stiff, and bossy

"The child is disoriented."

Step Five: The Whole Child

As we did previously, soft-focus on the picture you have built and then put it slightly to one side so that you can see the two visualizations, the child in the flow and in the fever, standing next to each other. Try to balance the two images so that neither dominates. In your mind's eye, look from one to the other: light and dark, levity and gravity, flow and fever.

This is the whole child. His or her struggles and sadnesess are as real and necessary as his or her successes. Take your time and, as best you can, look at them both with equanimity.

Moral Breathing in Practice

Many paths of self-development involve the conscious use of breath. In this phase of the Compassionate Response Practice, we will use the gesture of breathing but in a different way, a way that I call "Moral Breathing." As we have discussed in previous chapters, rather than focusing on the physical act of breathing in, you will take the visualization related to the emotional fever of the child and draw it toward you, moving it inward and integrating it. Then you will release in an outward direction the image of the child in flow. If this expansion and contraction happen to coincide with the natural rhythms of your breathing, it's perfectly fine, but try not to limit yourself to having the pictures you are working with comply with your physical breathing.

In this part of our practice you will see the term "heart's arms." It is used for release of the golden higher being and also for reaching out to the fevered self of the child. We have many terms that are similar, such as "our hearts leapt," "heavyhearted," and "heart's warmth," to name a few. This particular use of the phrase is not meant to relate only to our physical heart but to denote an expressive gesture of our deeper self. It is a gentle but powerful image that frees our feeling life from being a passive receiver of impressions and makes it possible to use it as an active helper of our intent.

You will also see the term "sea of compassion." This is a place in ourselves that we come to know primarily when a life-altering event occurs within our family or to our friends or, if you are an educator, to a child, parent, or colleague in your class or school. However, this vast, limitless, and deep space lives within us at all times. In this practice we open up pathways to this capacity without waiting for life's big occurrences to take us there. We then use it to cultivate compassion for a child, as this is what brings about one of the most important and elusive shifts every adult needs: forgiveness for the child.

Step One: Radiate

- Return your focus to the whole child. See both images, the child in flow and the child in fever, side by side.
- Open your heart's arms and welcome the flowing image you have created.

- Hold it close, but hold it lightly.
- Feel the cumulative warmth of the child's ease, resiliency, balance, and centeredness fill your chest.
- Take your time and allow the loving abundance you feel for this child to permeate you. Allow it to flow upward through your neck and head and downward through your lower body. As it does this, it grows not only in warmth but also in light.
- Embrace this light in your heart's arms and reach outward.
- Share it. Let it go, grow, and glow. Let it gently radiate all around you.
- Feel the calm, steady, and centering warmth you have created.

Step Two: Integrate

- With your heart's arms extended, reach out to the emotional-fever image of the child.
- Just as you would an unwell child, hold the struggling image with love, cradle it, and draw it toward you, but only as close as is comfortable.
- Look down on the emotionally fevered child. See him or her with care and quietness.
- The nearer he or she comes, the more the weight of emotions you have held lightens.
- As you draw the image closer, place it as a single drop in the vast sea of compassion you have within yourself.

- Quietly and slowly say to yourself, "I forgive."
- What was heavy is now light.
- What was restless is now still.
- What was disorienting is now centered.

Step Three: Radiate and Integrate

Repeat the above process at least two or three more times. With your heart's arms, first release and radiate the loving and centered image of the child in flow. Then draw the struggling, fevered child toward you and envelop it in your compassionate understanding.

Step Four: Unify

Now move the fevered child inward, just as you have been doing, but this time release the flowing child outward at the same time. If you can, allow the two to meet and merge. Don't worry if this does not happen at first. It's not easy. Take your time.

No longer separated . . .

> *Dark melds with light,*
> *Chaos melds with calm,*
> *Gravity melds with levity,*
> *Fever melds with flow.*

This is the child unified and whole.

Step Five: Closing

Maintain your quiet just a little longer. Let the experience of oneness you have created have the space it needs to be fully absorbed. If you feel words arise inside, listen to them and write them down when you are ready.

Likewise, if an image arises, give it space. These images and words are not ordinary. They come from a much deeper place. Some people have said that they feel they are "heaven sent" or "soul food"; others have simply commented that they are a "God-given gift." I like that one.

Sharing the Gift

If a motto or an image comes to you during the practice, consider sharing it with your partner, friends, or colleagues. Chat about what it may mean, much as you would when trying to figure out what a dream may have meant. The messages embedded in these images and words are often not as hard to understand as dreams, as they come from our consciousness rather than our sleep. They can be quite powerful and effective in uncovering a need and informing us of the best way to work with a child or a teen. If words came to you, try to distill them. I have heard lovely mottoes, like "I will bring you the warmth of the sun," "Yesterday is gone, today is new, and here we are," and "I am a safe harbor when your seas are stormy." Try to remember these special words as you greet and work with the child every day.

Here is one vivid example of an image that was easy to glean meaning from and was shared with others. I was once engaged in this practice with my high school faculty colleagues. As the subject of my meditation, I chose a sixteen-year-old girl whom I had known since she was young. She was from a very large family and was being raised by a hardworking single mother. There was not a lot of money in her life. Martha was the second to youngest of six children. She would spend a lot of time with her older brothers and sister and their friends. Over the years, she had been exposed to many things that were inappropriate for her age. Not surprisingly, but much to my concern, she had started attending raves (very large music-based gatherings of mainly younger adults where chemical drug use was common). I was not exactly sure what substance Martha was using, but she began to look very altered. Her long, dark, silky hair, which she usually kept beautifully, was going unwashed and becoming matted. She was paying little attention to the small collection of clothes she had always before put together with care to look fresh and fashionable. Emotionally she would either flare into raging outbursts or put her head on her desk in exhaustion. Her schoolwork was suffering. As well as being the school counselor, I was also the basketball coach of her girl's team and knew her to be a gifted, fair, and fast player who was dedicated to her teammates, but here again she began to falter, blowing off practice and arguing on the court.

Of course, the teachers were concerned, but some were disciplining her quite strongly. She was emotionally vulnerable and brittle, which was escalating an already difficult situation. After carrying Martha in the Compassionate Response Practice, an image of such clarity arose that I felt compelled to share it with my colleagues. This was something we would do from time to time, and they listened in with interest, because we all wanted some insight into how to care for this dear girl. The picture that came to me was that of a beautiful two-year-old filly freely galloping across an undulating grassy field. Her mane and tail were streaming behind her as she willed herself to stretch out and go ever faster. In my mind's eye I watched with an uplift of joy for Martha, as I knew this aspect of her being well. However, the image playing out before me shifted. I had been viewing the scene from an elevated vantage point, as if I was hovering above the young horse but keeping pace with her. Now my position rapidly shifted upward so that I was able to take in the whole scene. I saw that the field she was galloping through was bordered by a sea cliff. She was only a few feet away from the edge, and the sea foamed against the rocks far below. One small misstep would take her over the edge.

The faculty went quiet for a moment as we took in this harrowing picture. The first person to speak was the gruff but caring science teacher who had been a horsewoman in her younger days. In her straightforward, aristocratic British accent she said, "Well, we had all better pay bloody good attention not to spook her. Light on the rein. Can't keep up that pace for long without breaking down." The message was clear: Martha was close to the edge, and we needed to lead her away from the cliff face and help her slow down before she burned out.

In the weeks and months that followed, we all did what we could to give Martha more space. Teachers altered their work expectations a little and subtly affirmed the efforts she was making. Our colleague's warning "not to spook her" informed much of what we did yet left us free to make our own interpretation of the words. Most importantly, rather than putting Martha on academic or behavioral notice, we found a new way within ourselves to recognize the real trouble she was in and on a deeper level to reach out to her. I was so proud of the faculty.

Martha made it through to twelfth grade (not without some adventures) and graduated. She attended college and is now a well-respected kindergarten teacher. I can't help but suspect that her intense struggles, and perhaps the support she was given, helped her become the gifted and very empathetic educator she is today.

A Note to Educators and Care Professionals

A number of faculties and care teams have taken up the Compassionate Response Practice on a weekly basis. Each person quietly chooses a student or client he or she will carry. The group need not choose the same child. By doing this, many children are held in this very special way each week. The practice can be guided by someone who slowly reads the guidelines in this chapter out loud to the group. The whole process need only take about five to ten minutes to complete, and yet it can bring a palpable deepening of the work with the student body or clientele and especially with those children and teens in need.

During the practice, if words or images arise, faculty or care team members are encouraged to share these insights. If there is time, the group can briefly discuss what the images or words might mean to them and how the group might shift the way they will work with the student or client in question. The task is then taken up to apply the meaning of the images or words in the coming week. Each time a faculty or care team member comes into contact with the child, the adult tries to have the motto or image impressed upon them and be open to the shift in the way they work with the child or teen, small or large, that may occur. If the faculty or care team members meet regularly, the next time they gather, a brief amount of time can be spent checking in on the child's state, what changes each of the adults may have made, and what they have noticed.

PART THREE

THE TRANSFORMATION

The Gift of the Real You

In this section we consider the shifts in our lives that the Compassionate Response Practice brings. We will explore:

- A story of simple and deep change.
- How your interactions right in the moment can become calm and centered.
- How you can clearly see your child's intent rather than only his or her words or deeds.
- A whole new and widened range of emotional responses. From being very gentle to firm and clear, the choice is yours.
- The healing that comes with knowing how to make relational repairs.

14

Widening Your Range of
Emotional Responses

This promises to be an exciting chapter, because we explore the new possibilities that open up when we practice the strategies for becoming oriented and calm when squalls blow through our families. We all have ways of working with our kids, ways that for the most part are okay. We wouldn't have gotten this far in our family life unless we were doing something right at least some of the time.

However, it is liberating to discover we can have a much wider range of tools available to us than we thought, and that is just what you will see laid out in this chapter. It is like gifting one's self one of those big, impressive red toolbox cabinets that come with wheels so that you can roll them right to the place where you are working, with no heavy lifting needed. They are organized with elegant efficiency in mind: a few small drawers and storage compartments at the top for all the fine, lightweight tools; a larger selection of drawers for the midsized tools; and, finally, the impressive, deep drawers at the bottom for the heavy-duty tools. These are the kind of large tools that you rarely use, but when a pipe bursts and water is spraying all over the floor, having at hand a large multigrip and adjustable monkey wrench means you can minimize damage and get the water flowing again without a lot of panic.

Let's take a look at some of these tools you have gathered.

Reading What Your Body Tells You

Our bodies are always emotionally communicating with us— it's just that we don't often listen well enough. We may get the first part of the message, such as "I feel okay" or "This is an uncomfortable situation," as these come up many times each day. We either do more if the experience is good or change direction if it feels bad—an instinctive, primitive survival response.

Children, who live so strongly in their bodies, work things out in a similar way, at first with their sense of touch, when they intently explore everything they get hold of, and then later in their teens, when they go through many physical changes. It's a strange kind of morphing we need to support, from filtering all the nasty things that infants try to put *into* their mouths to helping them filter what comes *out* of their mouths when they are teenagers. However, the message from our children of any age is the same: "Please help me grow into this world." We become attuned to watching the cues their movements give us to find the possible reasons for their tears or frustrations. Being young, our kids tend to listen to the first part of the message the body sends them. As adults we can train ourselves to be more objective and inquisitive. What the Compassionate Response Practice helps us do is to expand our natural intuition into conscious awareness so we can listen to the whole message our body is giving us. This is especially important when things are headed into conflict.

Right in the moment when things are not going well with your child, the simple act of noticing—of watching from the balcony—as a familiar tension creeps into your body means that you are much less likely to get entangled in a web of reactive and unhelpful responses. After all, more than 70 percent of communication is nonverbal, and we can become aware of what our body is telling us just as we can become better at being conscious of hurtful or blaming words that form inside us *before* we speak.

Relaxed Body, Soft Eyes

We all know that our body language and facial expressions communicate many unspoken feelings to our children. This is even more true when our kids are upset and vulnerable. It is as if their normal protective layers fall away when they are distressed. One mother commented, "When my three-year-old does something she knows is not okay, she looks *right at me* to see what I am going to do. If I look even a little bit mad, she does a runner, and she is fast. If I keep it together, she stays around and looks a bit remorseful."

When we get hold of our frustrations and stay centered, our whole posture changes. It becomes upright without being rigid. Our posture tends to round off and relax into ease almost imperceptibly, which means

- Our knees don't lock and shove backward but float in a neutral way
- Our hands don't clench or arms cross but rest by our sides
- Our shoulders don't rise and contract but relax and broaden
- Our neck doesn't compact and shorten but slightly lengthens

Our face is affected similarly. It may not mean that we smile—after all, our child has just done or said something that is challenging—but our eyes may soften, slightly falling at the outer edges and gently enlarging. Our gaze becomes a bit peripheral rather than beaming in and fixing on the child. Our brow remains smooth, and the whole area around our eyes becomes malleable and warm. It's as if our eyes are saying, "Oh, dear . . . I love you but not what you did."

Calibrating Your Responses

His Holiness the Dalai Lama once famously said, "Be kind whenever possible. It's always possible." Whenever I think of him saying this, I feel his sense of humor as well as wisdom. If kindness were a mountain, there would be many paths to the top. Some are gently meandering forest trails; others are rocky and steep but direct. The same is true with our emotional responses to our family. There are times when we need to absorb the frustration of our children, when our caring and soothing presence is enough. In other situations we need to be strong, clear, and firm in showing that a line has been crossed. And, of course, there is everything in between these two polarities.

One of the main outcomes you will likely experience if you use the Compassionate Response Practice is that you will improve your ability to calibrate your responses. It is not that you have not had some good tools in your toolbox, but now you will be able to reach in and use them with confidence as well as have new ones available when needed. One father wrote to me in a quandary about his responses to his nine-year-old son. "I was determined to not be the stereotypical black male father, either angry or absent," he said. "I have a temper, and it never served me well, so I promised myself I would not raise my boy in a home with shame and fear. I wanted him to grow up to be a caring and considerate man. Even though I had to swallow a lot of bad behavior, I never shouted at him, not once. I thought I was doing okay, but now my wife is getting on my case because she feels I am giving way to him and she always has to be the bad guy. Added to that, she is getting worried that he is acting like a spoiled brat. I have to confess his behavior is not good, and I am confused at all his overentitled stuff and sassiness toward me, because I've tried so hard to be good to him. It is not working out like I had planned. Any ideas?"

In the weeks that followed, we met and explored the effects his "swallowing" his son's behavior had created. Sometimes it had led to him taking out his frustration on his wife, which resulted in an increasing number of angry exchanges. He also said his son was having a bit of trouble at school with his friends as well as with a few teachers. An important moment came when he blurted out with passion, "This promise to never shout is killing me, because sometimes that boy needs to be told plain and simple!" We explored the difference between destructive anger and constructive intensity. "Yeah, but what's to stop me from losing it? Because that could get ugly."

Many good parents have been in just this kind of dilemma. They tend to stay passive or hesitant when challenged by their kids because they have an intuitive dread that they will end up doing something regretful if they respond in any way. The common fears are that "I will be violent and hit my child or I will scream at them in an uncontrollable and truly intimidating way." Other concerns around more subtly destructive behavior, such as cutting sarcasm, put-downs, and rejection-based responses, also can cause parents to back off.

The Compassionate Response Practice enables us to deal with these well-based fears by accepting them as real rather than freezing in denial or guilt. And it goes one vital step further: it helps us to integrate them and in so doing it frees us to be able to be tender when gentleness is needed and firm when assertiveness is called for.

So what of the dad I mentioned earlier? He was very motivated on hearing there was a possible way out of the situation that was troubling him. "I took this practice seriously, as it made perfect sense to me," he said. "I did it every morning for just a minute or two before I hit the dreaded getting-out-the-door rush hour and then again at night before I went to bed. I was really surprised at how revealing it was about the anger I had been sitting on. In beginning this practice, I was aiming at being more of the assertive guy, and definitely not the angry dude, and that worked well. It took three or four times of my being strong, in the good way, but my boy got it and settled down. I was so pleased. It was like I pulled back the curtains and saw my fathering in a whole different way." Unexpectedly, the change in their father-son dynamic came with a beautiful bonus. "The thing that was a surprise was how my son started relating to me. In some way it was no big deal, it was just kind of normal. He began speaking in a regular way, no street or trash talk. It was like, because I had taken off my armor of self-protection, he could too." He finished by saying, "My wife told me that I was a good dad. I asked her if she would put that in writing, and we both laughed a lot . . . I'm still waiting for the note."

Emotional Muscle Memory

We practice for many of the events in life. If we are performing in a musical concert or have a role in a play, we rehearse until we feel confident of our performance. We take driving lessons and practice that elusive art of parallel parking before taking our test. If we play a sport, we usually engage in regular and sometimes intense training. One of the central aims of practice is to develop a dynamic called *muscle memory*, which causes us to automatically respond to any given situation appropriately, whether while driving or in the game. This can happen only if we prepare thoroughly by going over and over the skill we wish to acquire.

For many, the whole idea of practicing has been overlooked when it comes to human relationships and in particular the important area of parenting. But not for you! In part 1 of this book, we have explored what may have been derailing and triggering you in your relationship with your children. In part 2, you moved into the Compassionate Response Practice and by doing so you prepared for the inevitable challenges your kids will always put your way. The more you practice this exercise, the more satisfied and grounded you will become when your kids are disoriented. The most encouraging part is that your actions will increasingly come from your heart and not just from theory. As the months roll on and you continue to practice briefly each day, your trust in your ability to stay centered will build your quiet confidence that you can deal with all that family life is guaranteed to bring your way.

Opening a Relational Savings Account

True and enduring connection to our children is built interaction by interaction. Some people say, "Don't sweat the small stuff," but in family life, it is all about the small daily exchanges, both happy and hard. By identifying your parenting trigger points and learning how to integrate your frustrations, you will stand a very good chance of having many more healthy encounters than difficult ones.

In a workshop, a man who was involved in the financial world brought up a way of looking at his parenting that made us all laugh. He talked about all the small things we do to connect to our kids as forms of investment. The things you do today, he said, will have big payoffs in the future, when relations are strained or you have to step in and put limits on your son or daughter. In other words, in those tough moments you can draw on some of the credit you banked earlier. The good news is, there are many ways to build up your credit. Some are practical, like standing out in the freezing rain to cheer on your child playing soccer and taking her to her favorite pizza place afterward to warm up and chat easily about the game. Some are emotionally based credits that, over time, become high-yield investments. In a conflict, every time we lose it and shout, we pay out, and every time we stay centered and strong, we pay in. Because our kids learn about how to do this thing called life primarily by testing the limits, you are going to get lots of relational investment opportunities as they grow up. We ended the conversation in the workshop by agreeing that it was good to know there was a way to make sure we kept our balance healthy.

Inside Matches Outside

Kids have an unnerving ability to tell when we are being fake or being real. Although they don't know it, what they are doing is reading what is going on inside us and matching that up with what we are saying or doing on the outside. If the two line up, we are being real, and if they do not, then we are being fake. If the inner sense and outer action *really* misalign, then we are being "weird" or even "creepy." While these are not the most academically rigorous or technically accurate terms, they pretty much sum things up.

One father who was having a hard time with his family life said to me, "I am a straightforward kind of a guy. If my kids are acting out, I get angry. I can't help shouting, but then I get over it. At least my kids know where they stand." My response was, "Being straight is good, but wouldn't you rather be the calm guy who helps them work it out?" We talked about it for a while, and then he said, "I guess if I kept it together, I wouldn't have anything to get over, and my kids would like where I stand and maybe like *me*."

I remember driving a van load of fourteen- and fifteen-year-old girls back from a basketball game. They invented a game they called Calm Screaming: They would choose a teacher or parent, and then two girls would pretend to be this person. The first girl would make a comment in a nice but emotionally suppressed voice. For example, she might say, "Oh, Sara, I am more than a little disappointed," impersonating the adult. Then the second girl would scream at the top of her lungs what she imagined the adult's repressed feelings actually were: "I HATE IT WHEN YOU DO THAT, YOU STUPID PERSON!" The girls would convulse in laughter, and I have to admit it was pretty funny. When they had recovered themselves, they would select another adult victim and then, in a wickedly insightful caricature, repeat the same process. More uncontrolled laughter.

It was great that these older kids were able to joke about something they observed in adults, and as with all things truly funny, the game was very close to the truth. However, young children don't have this same ability. When they are met with an adult whose words do not match up with their feelings, they can feel unsafe. And small children tend to have an even sharper ability to know what is going on inside us. They seem to be clairsentient, which means they have a sixth sense to see inside another person's reactions. According to research on the brain development of young children, not only do they pick up on our inner life, but they also relive it within themselves. All this is natural and healthy, but it can cause intense confusion if a child is inwardly experiencing our anger as if it is very real but outwardly we are giving him the impression that everything is fine. The result is a child who gets the message that either he can't trust us or he cannot rely on his own perceptions. A child's main developmental questions in his early years are "Can I trust?" and "Am I safe?" Given this, we can seriously undermine our relationship and our child's ability to attach and bond with us if what we feel and what we say are mismatched.

So what does a child do if she has a dad who, while trying his best to control his frustration and speak normally, is setting off unconscious alarm bells? The answer lies in what has been learned from careful observation of animals in their natural habitats. For example, when a young gorilla senses threat, it will stand up high on its back legs and widen its ears and eyes to scan for danger. If the risk continues, either it will flee to the protection of the group if it's alone, it will prepare to fight, or, if all else fails, it will hide, making itself as small and still as possible. Our children go through similar phases when their insecurity is triggered. First their nervous systems go on high alert, and they anxiously try to take in as much information as possible. Next they may ping us with challenging behavior, as I described earlier. Finally, if the confusion continues, they will pull away from us and retreat inside themselves.

That could be a pretty revealing or maybe a depressing picture, but the very good news is that it doesn't have to be that way at all.

If you use the Compassionate Response Practice, it will come as no surprise to you that it offers a simple and clear way to work through a lot of your inner stuff—the very stuff that can set off your children's alarm bells. The more this practice becomes a part of your daily life, the less you have to try to suppress the rising red mists when challenging situations come up. You are learning to do this by being willing to recognize and explore what your struggles have been and opening yourself to assimilating the aspects of your relationship with your kids that in the past would have triggered you. This means your inside world will increasingly match your outer responses, and your kids will sense this and feel more and more secure and connected to you. Importantly, they will be able to rely on their own reading of you and your feelings, because what they hear you say and see you do will confirm for them that they were right and their world is good.

Balancing Heavy and Light

We often tend to allow the aspects of ourselves that are not so good and helpful to occupy too much inner real estate. The parts of us that are caring and quietly successful can become like a small, gated community within our emotional self. As a result, our responses tend to be dominated by our negative self-image. We can become defensive, aggressive, or even reckless as we justify or excuse our destructive behavior. Here is an example of this dynamic that also tells a bit of the history of the Compassionate Response Practice.

Early on in my counseling career, I was struggling to find a way to help fathers who were perpetators of domestic abuse. These men had been through a lot of different anger management classes where they would often do well at the time, but once back in the real-world home environment, they would get triggered and fall back into emotionally or physically abusive behavior. When I would carefully listen to these stories, two outstanding patterns began to emerge. First, they tended to see their family members mainly through a fixed perspective. They would say things like, "I have no trouble with my oldest boy. He is a good kid, but my daughter is defiant and sassy all the time," or, "My wife is mean and criticizes every thing I do, no matter what!" The more rigid their view of the family member, the deeper the problem.

Second, just about all of these men carried a deep sorrow and guilt over their actions and the hurt they had caused. They tended to push away and deny their emotions and struggled to come to terms with the shame they experienced. The men understandably did not want to talk about this, saying things like, "Yes, I am a bad person and that is about all there is to it." This took some time to break through, but it always began to occur when I turned the conversation to their positive qualities.

Initially when I asked them about the good they brought their children and wives, they often looked surprised at the question. Some had real difficulty in remembering a single positive attribute about themselves as fathers or husbands/partners, and those that could would often say things like, "Oh, being able to do that is no big deal." It occured to me that these positive characteristics were wonderful and full of light, but there was simply not enough space in their emotional self due to the darkness of their shame feeling so large and all-consuming. They would talk about playing ball or just hanging out with their kids, being funny or loving, tender, attentive and protective. Of course, the harsh things they had done were very real, but still, all these great qualities that were being dismissed needed to be given more credence.

It seemed to me that these gentlemen (yes, they had gentleness in their soul) first had to be helped to unlock their fixed way of viewing those around them. On top of this, they needed to recognize their fine, essential capacities. An emotional balance had to be created not only because that is healthy, but also because they needed to believe in themselves again. The goodness in each family member, including themselves, needed more space and recognition.

In the years of working in this very simple way, very few of these men ever reoffended. Right at the heart of it was a need to see that their children and partners had beauty within them as well as behavior that was difficult. In doing this they found a way to lift themselves out of the very narrow, dominant, and destructive habit of reactivity and into a much more expanded, calm, and balanced response to the day-to-day parenting situations that in the past would have triggered them.

Uncovering Your Voice

One of these men, who had been struggling for years with his anger and working with the practice, turned up unexpectedly at my office one day. I was happy to see him as he had, in the past, been reluctant to come to our meetings. He said that he had to talk and looked excited. "You know I have had a really messed-up past, like when I was a kid I got treated bad and that really got inside me," he started. "But something has changed big time." He sat down on the edge of a chair and recounted this story.

"It just happened yesterday afternoon, and I have just got to tell you about it because you will understand. It was the end of a long day, and my daughter was flat refusing to get in the car. I knew and she knew that we were headed into really dangerous territory. And then it happened. It's hard to describe how good it felt, but I was able to speak to my child knowing that it was *me* she was hearing and not something from my messed-up past. I kept it cool and all that, but that is not what was amazing. I told her, right there outside the car, that I loved her more than she would ever know and how she was so often a lot of fun—she's got a great sense of humor—but she was going to help now because we needed to get to her mother's house on time because that is what I said I would do. 'I do what I say, baby, and this is one of those times.'" He paused and nodded his head. "The words that I spoke sounded like they came from someplace either way inside me or way above—I couldn't really tell—but they were different, really different. I know this sounds strange, but I have never really heard my real voice before, not like that. Now that I know what it sounds like, I am sure I can do it again. Okay, that's it." We stood quietly for an extended moment, and even though it was a bit out of the ordinary, we hugged. Then he left, only to pop back through the door a few seconds later saying, "Oh, she got right in the car, buckled herself up—that's always been a big problem—and we sang silly songs all the way to her mom's house. You know, when she got out of the car I just cried."

Practice Involves Practice

Our kids have triggered us so many times that as a result we very likely have developed some unhelpful habits in our responses. Negative habits are stubborn things to change, because they come mainly from our unresolved past and sneak into our unconscious actions. In order to transform an unwanted reflexive response into a new, healthy emotional muscle memory, you will need to engage in the Compassionate Response Practice pretty much daily for a month or so.

Think of yourself like a tennis player who has suffered a repetitive strain injury to her elbow. She is well known for a fast and powerful serve that intimidates her opponents, but she has developed a habit of overtensing her arm to hit the ball hard. The physical therapist has had her watch a video showing the mechanics of her problematic movement. She has carefully constructed a new way to serve that is more relaxed and extended. However, she worries that she will not have the same power as before, as the new technique feels too loose and easy. Before she can roll this revised serve out in a tournament, she practices it over and over, at first carefully and consciously breaking it down into its component parts. It feels strange to begin with, and she works hard to stay focused in order to not fall back into old habits that somehow feel more effective even though she knows they will cause her pain. Slowly, the new way becomes normal, something she doesn't have to think about. Come game day, to her surprise and joy, her new, flowing serve is more than fifteen miles per hour faster and much more controlled and accurate than the old serve. She almost doubles the number of aces she serves. This story is not just a good metaphor; it is a true account that comes from a Spacial Dynamics physical therapist.

Here's how the situation of the tennis player relates to our parenting. You may have worked yourself into old habits of relating to your kids when they pushed your buttons that were forceful, to some extent effective, but not sustainable. In part 1 of this book we looked at why you may have developed these unhelpful habits and explored what was wrong with them. In part 2, you carefully constructed a new, more compassionate way of responding and began to quietly practice it. According to the feedback of countless parents, it usually takes around three to four weeks of practicing the visualization exercise in order for it to be ready for game time with your kids. In a fast-moving world, inwardly rehearsing something for three or more weeks can seem like a lot to do, but such a practice actually delivers a very good return on your time. Let's do the math. The number of occasions you have been triggered to a greater or lesser extent probably adds up to the many hundreds (as disconcerting as that is). Engaging in the Compassionate Response Practice for a minute or two a couple of times a day for three or four weeks involves between forty and fifty brief focused sessions. In other words, we are undoing in three or four weeks what has been tripping us up for years. It's tempting to say this is a good deal, but we are not buying and selling: we are working to give our children a safe and connected family life, which is at the heart of what every parent wants for his or her child.

Moreover, actively engaging in this process lessens the feeling that outside forces are somehow preventing us from being happy and instead offers us a path to do something practical and powerful about taking back control, bringing us closer each day to living in alignment with our hopes and dreams for our family life.

15

The Outcomes

Difficulties can blow up quickly with kids. You can be having a regular day, your child playing or engaged in some activity and you finally making a dent in your long-overdue housework. Maybe some small frustration results in your daughter making what sounds like a demand that you help her, "Now!" You ask her to wait, as you have already taken a lot of time to help her set up the things she needs for her project. She gets pushy, and you tell her you will be there "in just a *minute*," only now there is an edge of annoyance in your voice. She shouts from the other room, "Fine!" and throws something down that sounds very much like your good pair of scissors, which you gave to her to use on the promise she would be careful with them. Next, your child comes stomping into the room and throws herself on the sofa and knocks over the pile of laundry you were folding. Your eyes harden as you wonder if she did it on purpose.

Here's where something new can happen. You sense the familiar red mists of fever start to rise as you continue your housework, but rather than tensing your body and bracing for the looming ugly argument, you notice the tightening of your body and the building irritation of your mind. It's as if you are standing on the balcony watching the movement on the dance floor below. You recognize the annoyance is growing, and before you respond in any way, you breathe in the frustration and release out your centeredness. You can do this because it is exactly what you have been practicing for the last few weeks.

It's the first sign that this healthier response may be becoming the emotional muscle you were hoping for. Your eyes soften, a subtle ripple of relaxation runs down your body, and suddenly the *real you* that you want to be is standing in the room. Your child is looking at you, waiting to see what is going to happen. She senses something in you that if she had the words to put to it she might describe as "My mother is not mad and scary. She is strong and kind." You tell your child that it is hard to have something not go the way you want it to when you are working on a project. You remind her that she made a great board game last week that was such fun for everybody to play. But with firmness you tell her that it is absolutely *not* okay to mistreat precious tools.

You notice from your balcony that the voice you are speaking in is yours—yes, the one you knew was possible but so often got buried underneath complicated layers of emotional reactions. Your daughter is still upset, but where she would normally have been fiery or fresh, she says in a softer tone, "Well, I didn't mean it." You respond, "I know you didn't mean it. After we pick up these clothes and fold the last few socks, let's go and look at what went wrong." As you walk with her into the room where she had been working, a feeling of gentle elation fills you, and it only grows as you help her solve her problem. As you get back to your chores and pick up the laundry basket, you can't help but notice how different that small but important interaction felt.

In the Moment

To some of the parentally uninitiated, this story might seem like it was no big deal. Maybe it would appear that this mom kept her cool, and that's good, but to those of us who have lived every day wanting to be the best we can be with our kids and yet so often seem to fall short, it represents a seismic shift. This is the stuff of building care and connection with our family, one situation at a time. Certainly these steps of flow and fever visualization we have worked with are the vital foundations we stand on to know ourselves better as parents, but the real value of taking the time to practice is the lived experience of breaking out of unwanted patterns of disconnecting exchanges with our children. It would be great (and more than a little weird) if we could tell our kids, "Okay, hold that shockingly unfair accusation you are leveling at me. I need to meditate for a while, and I'll get back to you when I am done."

A study on sacred experiences led by Jaime Kucinskas, an assistant sociology professor at Hamilton College in Clinton, New York, found strong evidence challenging the traditional view that spiritual experiences tend to occur rarely and in isolation. Her team's findings tell us that "special sacred and meaningful moments tend to occur in the midst of people's daily activities, rather than when they are alone, at rest." As parents we know there are very few moments when we have quiet and alone time, so this information is good news. The even better news is that we don't have to wait for random experiences of relevance. Through our simple but conscious preparation, we can significantly increase our ability to be truly present, so that an interaction with our children can move from the mundane to the meaningful. Then in the evening, when we look back on our day, we can see waypoints of connection that gave the day its healthy shape. Cultivating the ability to stay centered when our children are losing it is just as sacred and special as the lovely and fun times. At the heart of many accounts in sacred texts from all spiritual paths are stories of helping the vulnerable and the suffering. Few moms or dads will claim saintly status for helping our kids when they need us, but each time we do, we bring a small blessing down on our family that feels whole, holy, and good.

A Meditation in Real Time

Many meditative practices help us know ourselves better. They are meant to assist us in our search for the spiritual dimensions inside. However, more and more I have come to see that the holy is moving from *within* us to *between* us. Even the word *meditate* has its roots in the concept of finding the middle ground. In this sense the quiet, solitary practice of meditation melds with the problem-solving quality of mediation. As the Roman Catholic tradition of the Eucharist carries the message of transubstantiation, through which the essence of bread and wine becomes the body and blood of Christ, many spiritual rites represent change.

What is held in ritual can also be brought into daily reality when we consciously take hold of a potentially angry exchange with our son or daughter (or any person) and transform it into a new way of being together. Rudolf Steiner put it clearly when he said:

In the future no human being is to find peace in the enjoyment of happiness if others beside him are unhappy. . . . Every human being shall see in each and all of his fellow mankind a hidden divinity . . . that every human being is made in the likeness of the Godhead. When that time comes, every meeting between one person and another will of itself be in the nature of a religious rite, a sacrament.

Our children are the most precious things in our lives, so it makes perfect sense that we pay special attention to having what flows between us each day be a small secret sacrament. To subtly spiritualize the ordinary is to bring grace into a home. Our children can sense this without having the words to express it.

The Gift of Noticing

Being present allows you to notice things you very likely overlooked previously. Many of us are familiar with the saying "Don't just stand there, do something." Another way of looking at it is "Don't just do something, be there." When things are not going well with our kids, there are often all sorts of emotional currents churning about inside us. Understandably, our attention goes to trying to sort these moods out, and that means our focus can get caught on our inner process. Trying to figure out our feelings is fine, but in everyday family life, situations can blow up. If we can process our inner stuff quickly, we can clear our vision to look at what is happening with our child and come up with a response that will de-escalate the problem and keep the day moving along.

Intention

So what happens when we find a way to tame the emotional tumult that often arises when our kids push our buttons? The answer is that we gift ourselves the power to notice, and in doing so we come to understand that behavior is communication, nothing more, nothing less. Something vital to a healthy relationship is now revealed to us: the intention of the child.

First, if you are using the Compassionate Response Practice, it is now very unlikely that you will get caught up in the behavior itself. You can look with soft eyes at your son and remember how vulnerable he is when he is upset, hurt, or angry. He is peeling back his emotional layers, and you can stay calmly in the moment by drawing in any feelings of frustration and expanding outward your feelings of centeredness.

Now you have a far better chance of becoming attuned to what the true intention of your child or teen might be. Your young son may be raging and throwing things off the table, but his intention was to create a drawing of an animal he saw that he wanted to show you, and he is frustrated that it looks "dumb." His intention was to share something special with you and to show you what you missed seeing. Your teenage daughter may be sullen and grumpy when you remind her that she seriously needs to tidy her room. Her intention was to get to it after supper, put on some of her favorite songs, and spend the whole evening on the task so that she wouldn't have to hurry and feel forced. Your toddler erupts in anger when you take the silk cloth he gives you, fold it, and put it away in a basket. His intention was to have you feel how soft it was against your face.

Even if the child's exact intention is not apparent right away, stilling yourself and being present allows the child to open to you a little more. It is then that you can begin to catch a glimpse of what the real problem might be.

From Self-Control to Coregulation

It is so pleasing when your child begins to develop more self-control and learns to solve problems with less help than before. It was a relief when my eldest daughter first began to get over her frustrations. I would sit with her as she tried to figure things out. It is always a balancing act to avoid overhelping but not be too detached. If a child feels emotionally lost, she needs us to have the composure to help her find herself again. It was heartwarming to hear her exclaim, "*I did it, Daddy, all by my own!*"

Of course, the fast track to children developing self-control is if the adults around them are centered and well oriented. On a behavioral level, we are aware that modeling self-control is required if we want our kids to do the same. Maybe that's all we need to know, but I remember a major "a-ha!" moment when I first came across the brain-based science around what is known as *mirror neurons*. Scientific findings suggest that the neurons that fire in our brain when we are physically *performing* an action are the same neurons that fire when we *observe* someone else doing the same action. However, one of the most powerful roles suggested for the mirror-neuron system in humans is that it may help us understand not just other people's physical actions or even speech but also their minds and their intentions.

This means that when an adult stays centered, even when a child is upset, the mirror-neuron activity in the child's brain will sense our calm and start to copy it. The child now has a pathway out of his meltdown via coregulating with a caring adult.

Two Hearts Beat as One

Another moving scientific finding that strongly validates what the Compassionate Response Practice can bring comes from the late human and child development expert Joseph Chilton Pearce. Here is what the author said in his interview for the communications platform Touch the Future:

> Now if we look at the connection with the heart, we get into some very interesting research. I've talked about the intelligence of the heart. Of course, everyone assumes that this is a metaphor, and it is a metaphor, but it is also a fact. You can take a heart cell out of the heart and put it in the right kind of a fluid and keep it alive for a while.
>
> The interesting thing about the heart cell disconnected from the heart was that it quickly lost its rhythmic pulsation and began to fibrillate. It would just flop all around out of rhythm and soon destroy itself and die. Put two heart cells together on the slide, and they will both fibrillate in that fashion. The poor little creature can't stand to be cut off from its matrix, from its source. And neither can we. If we are cut off from our heart, we fibrillate; it just takes us a

little longer to die. Now the interesting thing about these two heart cells is, if you bring them close enough together, at a certain point of spatial proximity, they do not have to touch. There can be a physical barrier between them, but at a certain point of spatial proximity, the two heart cells somehow or other communicate with one another and immediately go back into the synchronous rhythm which they experienced within the heart itself.

I was attending a lecture when Dr. Chilton Pearce spoke of this finding. There was a quiet but audible gasp around the audience as we all took in the meaning of his words. If an isolated and dying heart cell can be brought back to life and pulse with another only if the second cell comes close, the parallels for our parenting an upset child are very clear. Shouting or angrily sending our daughter to her room is an unfortunate demonstration of rejection-based discipline and isolation, and it results in emotional fibrillation. However, if we can stay regulated enough to not follow her into reactive spasm but rather keep the steady beat of our care for her, we can bring her back to herself again and in doing so bond on a foundational level.

16

Values Centered versus Child Centered

Having a child-centered family sounds reasonable and loving. However, sometimes the term *child centered* seems to be code for "child led." Very well-meaning parents whose intention is to be kind and caring inadvertently set themselves up to be dominated by a child. One dad laughed ruefully as he said that he had become a "courtier to a child emperor." Giving kids this much influence and power is demanding for the whole family—and, counterintuitively, very stressful for the child. When children are placed in this role, their actions seem tinged with desperation as they give their unrealistic orders and become furious when they are not carried out to their satisfaction. The more that parents in this situation try to figure out what is wrong with their son or daughter, the worse things seem to get.

The answer often lies in a change of direction. Simply put, values need to be at the center of our family, not children. It is important and healthy to move our thinking away from being singularly focused on a child's needs and toward clarifying and standing on our parental beliefs of what is healthy for our kids and for ourselves. These core ethics need to be at the heart of our family, and when they are, our kids sense it and feel secure.

A values-centered family has a deep well from which everyone can refresh and renew themselves when things get tough or complicated. This offers two long-term payoffs. First, when children are out of the house and not directly under your influence, all sorts of temptations will come their way, and they will have to make their own decisions. Do they go along with the group and pick on the new kid in the class, or do they quietly support the new student? Do they join in with some shoplifting, or do they walk away? Do they smoke the joint that is being passed around, or do they discreetly pass it on without using it? Second, when your kids are grown and have their own independent lives, the good, rich soil of the values you worked to give them will help the seeds of their own virtues take strong root.

From Little Things Big Things Grow

The word *values* suggests the notion of something big, deep, and philosophical. It ranks up there with *truth* and *integrity*.

However, these ways in which we hope to live our lives and raise our families are built through all the small daily encounters we have with our kids. Pretty much every day, our kids push the limits in some way; how we respond to each request clarifies what our family stands for. Over time, something may emerge that is definable.

Here's an example. I coached high school basketball for many years. In a preseason practice, I once overheard a group of friends questioning why their best players had not been given much more court time than the others in the previous year. One player said, "I know it's important to win—I get that—but I grew up believing that it's about giving everyone a go who works hard. So for me it's as much about attitude as it is about how good you are with the ball." Later, when we were cleaning up after training, I asked the boy about his comment. "Yeah, that attitude thing is just one of those things my parents said over and over. Sometimes it was annoying, but I guess it got into me." I said, "How is that for you?" He gave a small shrug and with a quiet smile answered, "I guess I like it." I made him captain, and his approach had a very positive influence on the team. He didn't seem to dwell on this way of being. It was just who he was.

We did well that season, and after a big playoff game in which his leadership played a big part, I happened to catch up with his parents. I told them he had articulated that attitudes were an important factor in a game and that he had picked this up from them. They both were wide-eyed and smiling broadly when they said, "Well, who would have known! He used to push back pretty hard and tell us we were being boring, but we never let up." They left the gym that day looking like two very happy parents.

Uncovering Values

Many parents have been left bewildered by what they feel is their child's repeated bad behavior. While it's valuable sometimes to sit your kids down and seriously tell them about what is important to you, the big talk goes only so far. In my book *The Soul of Discipline* I write about "discipline as a definer of family values," and the metaphor I use is that of Michelangelo carving the statue of David. When he was asked how he was able to carve such a magnificent sculpture, he answered that he did not *carve it,* he took away that which was *not of David*. He went on to recount how this image also had to adapt to the contours and the grain of the stone and how the marble spoke to him. In other words, he had a clear image of what the statue would be, and he chipped away at it to reveal the visualization he inwardly had, but he also had to work with the demands made by the raw material of the stone. My point here is that what Michelangelo did is similar to being an effective parent. We can ponder what is going to be the bedrock of the way in which our family works, and that is a very good thing to do. Of course, qualities such as kindness and consideration, empathy and being true to yourself are probably on most parents' lists, but these are arrived at by the same kind of chipping away over the years that Michelangelo must have done in his studio. Our workshop is our family, and each time one of us speaks or acts in a way that doesn't feel right, we can correct it and take another step toward clarifying what we stand for. Just like the grain of the sculptor's marble, our children all have their individual characters and temperaments, which we work with each day, but what gives us our overall shape as a family—what provides us direction, particularly when difficulties arise—is the deeper vision of what we are striving to create.

Begin with the End in Mind

All through this book we have used the power of imagination and visualization. We first create a mental image and then use the power of the picture on a practical level. It's similar to designing a house: initially you work with an architect, and then you hand the design to the builders who will construct the home. Without the architect's blueprints, the contractors will likely make all sorts of decisions you did not see coming, and the house you end up living in will likely not be what you had in mind. Having a clear vision of what you want means that other people's ideas do not overpower you. This is particularly important in raising a family, as many dubious influences can take you and your kids away from where you want to be and how you want to live.

Slowing down to take stock of our morals and ethics and to consider how they express themselves in our family life gives us a vehicle by which to manifest, on a daily basis, our hopes for our kids' lives. In this way we are not only beginning with the end in mind—we are making that come true each day.

Knowing Your Place in the Order

Children thrive on form. Recently, at a farmers market, I watched as members of three generations from one family interacted with one another. The grandmother was clearly in charge of the baked goods and preserves they had for sale; the father was overseeing the vegetables. Both adults would answer market goers' questions about their produce in a knowledgeable and friendly way that gave the customers the confidence to buy. It was a busy scene, and their products sold very well. The two children were making sure that both tables were kept well stocked and that the area was tidy by clearing away boxes and stacking them in the van. They also were responsible for receiving money and making the correct change when their father and grandmother would hand them the customer's cash.

The children were well known to some of the regular attendees and would give happy waves and smiles when they were greeted. The whole system was smooth; everyone knew his or her job. But there was something more than organization going on: it was clarity about who had the background and skills to do what was appropriate. The authority was not forced; it was simple and natural. I wondered what would have happened if the roles had been reversed, with the children in charge of interacting with the customers and the adults assisting them. Some people may have found it "cute" (whenever I hear that word used about children, it is often code for "developmentally inappropriate"), but the kids almost certainly would not have given the public the confidence to purchase their goods; the wisdom and experience of the adults would have been underused; and the whole venture would have not reached its potential, resulting in vegetables and cakes left unsold.

Likewise, in our families children benefit from knowing where they stand. This is not in any way to suggest that we want children to feel subjugated and put down. The whole concept of *place* runs deep; it is what gives us our identity. Having children know their right place is to give them security and prevent them from becoming emotionally rootless.

Extended Family, Friends, and Other Weird Influences

Values travel well and can come to the rescue especially effectively at times when well-meaning, unthinking, or perhaps just plain stubborn people who are close to you seem to have the ability to challenge, ignore, and generally upset every boundary you have so carefully worked to instill in your kids. Rather than feel that the glue holding your family together is cracking, you can choose the much stronger practice of leaning into the long-fostered practices and understandings you have cultivated. This way you can keep the situation in the difficult-but-rescuable range and prevent it from lurching into possibly feral territory.

Contrast this kind of family dynamic with one that is child centered. Every family has a naughty uncle who seems to derive slightly perverse pleasure in giving your child sneaky access to very questionable amounts of unrefined media and highly refined sugar. If you have raised your kids to feel they are at the center of things—that their needs are paramount—and they get this kind of baited attention, the chances they have of hesitating over what is being offered is definitely not high. Moreover, it's unfair to place the burden of a moral dilemma like this one on a child.

If you are visiting with good people who live their lives differently than you do, you will likely need to be a diplomat when you diverge on how to handle situations that arise with the kids, and that seems reasonable. What feels wrong is when you feel the need to become a defender or an apologist for the way you are raising your kids. It's not much better when, in an attempt to just get through it, you try to swallow your disbelief and rising anger over what your extended family is doing.

When you are standing on solid family values, things can be different. Here are some outcomes that I have personally experienced and also many parents have commented on.

- When you speak about what is and is not okay to give your kids, your voice will have a ring of quiet but firm authenticity. This helps prevent you from seeming weak and pleading or forceful and unreasonable.

- You're much more likely to be proactive and set the boundaries before the visit, both with your kids and especially with your extended family or friends.
- Your kids see you as being "real." Superficially, they might not like that they don't get to play violent video games for hours, but they will respect you for standing on your beliefs.
- You avoid bursting out in angry recriminations against your extended family when you are driving home, which could embarrass and confuse your kids. Such outbursts may lead them to feel they have to choose between you and their "fun" family member.
- You can keep some basic understandings of "how we live no matter where we are." This is a very healthy message; over the long term, it communicates to your kids that they can stand up for what they believe in, even when others try to undermine them.
- You won't need to spend the coming days grumpily picking up the pieces that resulted from the visit. Dealing with an overwhelmed and sobbing child who seemed a few hours earlier to be having SO much fun is not fair to anyone.

It's true for most of us that when we were kids our own parents tried to raise us to have good manners and live a moral life. So when your children's grandparents either directly or furtively challenge your way of bringing your kids up, I think it is fair to say to them, "Look, you raised me to have values, so thank you, because I do. I know my way of doing things with my kids might not be the way you would do it, but they are my values, and they are strong and are not going to change . . . so really, it is your fault." Even though this can be said with a wry smile, it is true.

Finally, here is a great example of how sticking to your family virtues can work out. "We have always been pretty basic in the way we raise our kids," a dad wrote to me. "Of course, we are loving parents and have a lot of fun with our two sons (aged 7 and 9), but they know who is in charge. They push the limits just like any kids, but my wife and I both let them know over and over that being respectful, contributing to our home, and taking care of each other is what our family stands for. We feel that it is way easier to have some firm agreements about what is important and stick to them. Maybe that's a bit simplistic, but it works for us.

"My brother-in-law and sister are good people, but for years I could tell they didn't agree with us. They would often make little comments about how strict we were, and how our boys had too many jobs around the house and needed more freedom. They weren't in our face about it, but it was pretty continuous and obvious.

"One day my brother-in-law came over to check out our new woodstove. We had only had it a couple of weeks, but we had taught our kids how to help split and haul in wood, load the stove, and light the fire. As he was leaving, my brother-in-law said to me, 'You know, I am impressed. You showed your kids how to handle the stove, and they do just like you told them. Other parents I know would have fireguards and all sorts of stuff, and everyone would be anxious, but your kids are safe because they listen to you. I know I have sometimes thought you were a bit strict, but maybe I can see why, as they are turning out okay.' It was a busy day so I didn't get to tell my wife about what her brother had said until later that night. I must have been smiling a lot, because she said in a good-humored, dry way, 'Yeah, that is good, really, but I hope that means he will also stop buying them donuts right before supper.'"

Discovering Me 2.0

After a workshop on emotional self-regulation, a mom wrote in her journal, "I could never really put my finger on what it was that was missing when I became a mother. I adored my babies and our new life together, and I was okay, but as they grew up I was getting worn down." She continued, "I was doing the 'putting them first' thing, and the longer it went on, the more I felt like I was losing track of who I was. . . . When I came across the [Compassionate Response] practice I began to find myself again and what I stood for. Before I was a parent I did my best to be a nice person in general, but after going through this practice I realized that the *me* I had become was so much more capable and willing to take risks in giving my children the boundaries they need. It felt strange at first, because rather than following my kids around each day, wondering how to help them, I started setting up the day for them to follow. I was not sure if they would go along with it, but they did and were way happier. Sometimes the shape of family is defined as much by what you choose not to do as what you actually do. The piece that I have discovered is that it all starts with living the life you want with your kids and staying close to it."

Shifting from being child centered to value centered is a subtle process, yet it becomes increasingly powerful as you become more efficient and effective at it. I think of this as soul economy. Your kids will notice the change, though that is not the primary motivation. What is more important is that you are strengthening the core from which you make all the myriad small decisions that are asked of every parent. At the end of the day, chances are you will still be tired, but you will feel less of that awful, drained depletion and more of an experience of having stayed close to your values. In following that path you will find that only good things happen.

17

Making the Repair

Up to now we have been focused on making our responses centered and compassionate right in the moment when our kids are losing it. But what if you are not at your best and don't handle a situation well? The Compassionate Response Practice can also help us heal a situation after it has escalated and resulted in either an angry outburst or steely, pointed silence.

Compassion Does Not Have a Time Limit

Let's say your kid really got under your skin one day. Even though you have been doing well with the Compassionate Response Practice in most situations, you blow it, neglect dealing with your frustration, and instead shout or storm off angrily. Does this mean you are thrown all the way back to where you started, like some Snakes and Ladders–inspired anxiety dream? Certainly not. The key to healing this kind of situation, which so many of us have experienced, is to make the repair in a timely way. One mother commented that she was able to do this almost immediately after she let her anger get the better of her, and this is impressive. Most of us are going to need time to let our adrenaline and cortisol drain down before we can begin to inwardly organize ourselves and then go back to our child to patch things up. It usually takes about fifteen to twenty minutes to get our biochemical and emotional equilibrium back. What is important is to let your kids know that you are frustrated and need some space to get yourself back together. Parents will often say something to the effect of "I am going to take a quiet few minutes now. We'll come back to this soon, when we are all feeling a bit better," or simply "I need some space now." One father would tell his kids, in a nice piece of self-deprecating humor, "Don't poke the angry bear."

That said, it is vital to make the repair as soon as you are able. If your child had a physical cut that was bleeding, you would put some antiseptic cream and a Band-Aid on it as soon as possible to prevent infection. The same is true with an emotional wound, which is what has been sustained by both your child and you because of the situation that got out of hand between you.

One mother of three children wrote in with an intense example of how repair is still possible even in the long term. "It was not so much that I would shout and scream; I would go scarily silent and become rigid with anger. I would flatly refuse to communicate," she recounted. "Everyone would avoid me, and it took at least a couple of days of storm clouds hanging over the family for me to recover. It was a very lonely place for me to be in. This pattern went on for years before my oldest teenage daughter called me out. She told me that while I might eventually get over it and move on, she did not. She told me that when she was little she was afraid every time it happened that I was not going to come back and that it was her fault, and she would be left alone in the world. She said that no matter how many times it happened, this was her experience. It led to her having anxiety issues, and each time I went silent she put up more and more of a protective barrier between us. I told her it reminded me of that Pink Floyd song 'Another Brick in the Wall.' She had never heard of it, so I sheepishly sang her the small part I knew: "All in all it's just another brick in the wall.' She burst out crying and said that it was exactly what it was like. I promised her that there would be no more bricks."

There were specific reasons that such a good person had gotten herself into this situation, the main one being a reactive former husband who led her to repress her feelings and self-expression, especially in the home. At first she had explored what was derailing her, remembering and accepting that she was a kind and very loving mother. Then relations really began to improve with her children when she made it a daily practice to accept her shortfalls and celebrate her goodness. She finished her email by saying, "I was so relieved that I could still heal my relationship with my daughters, even after years of not doing well. If bricks can be put in the wall one by one, I can remove them in the same way, and I am doing it and my kids are coming back to me."

Being Okay with Messing Up

I once asked a group of teenagers why reality TV was so popular, and they looked at me as if I really didn't get it. Their answer was clear: "Because those gross things are happening to someone else and not happening to us." Everyone laughed as this dark truth was spoken out loud. But in parenting it *will* happen and *is* happening to us. Parenting does ask us to soften our self-judgments and see clearly that we are doing our best as well as making subtle or spectacular, colorful, and often public blunders. The ERIC principle is something to consider in this regard. I happened to see this on a classroom wall while I was visiting the Wasatch Charter School in Salt Lake City and was struck by its simple power. The ERIC principle states that mistakes are to be

E   Expected

R   Respected

I   Inspected

C   Corrected

The Compassionate Response Practice that has been laid out in this book is one powerful way to lessen the fear of making large and small parenting gaffes. It is only natural to be anxious about getting it wrong if there are no simple ways to put it right that are within your control and ability. Being able to laugh at your mistakes and not try to justify or cover them up is not only a healthy way to live but also very good role modeling for your kids. If your children are going to be at *their* best, they need to be okay with taking appropriate risks and accepting failure as a possibility. This is the basis of the crucial life skill called "grit." I hope you are coming to see and personally experience that you can relax a little and accept your fallibilities, explore why they have been coming up, and rest assured that you now have specific tools with which to make any necessary repairs.

Making the Course Corrections

When the mythological hero Jason first set sail with his crew of Argonauts, his goal was to find the golden fleece. In this story from ancient Greek times, we are told that his path was by no means straight and direct: his journey was fraught with a series of miscalculations, incidents of steering off course and making required corrections. In his wanderings he visited many strange lands and had perilous adventures, and he had to call on all his resources to guide him and his crew safely on. Moments of self-doubt arose, followed by elation when riddles were solved and dangers were surmounted. Each time he grew a little wiser, but not so wise that he did not have to struggle to find an answer to the next situation that he encountered. All the while Jason kept his vessel moving forward toward his goal.

When I first encountered this interpretation of the Argonauts story, it strongly reminded me of the path of parenting. While we have our hopes for our children and see within them potentials that we try to cultivate, we seldom follow a straight and direct path. Raising a child is much more like a series of course corrections, in which we realize we are drifting away from our goal and make adjustments to get back to where we need to be. This is what propels us forward and prevents us from stagnating and becoming rigid or vain. While this is not exactly a groundbreaking realization, few other aspects of life equal parenting as a practical, daily expression of this idea.

However, we are in trouble in contemporary society. We increasingly see struggle and discomfort as things to be avoided. If we are not perfectly well oriented at all times, something must be wrong. We then avoid the situation that causes us disorientation, or we conceal it and hope that it will go away; in either case we miss the vital learning experience offered to us. More importantly, we miss the chance to correct our course, and we veer further and further away from our goals and true intentions. What might have been a fleetingly uncomfortable recorrection becomes an emotionally turbulent challenge with extreme consequences, because we have gone so far off course that the correction is much more difficult than it need be. We can prevent having to make these very large, painful corrections by fully facing the small but nevertheless painful moments in our parenting and using the tools we've learned to explore what is happening.

Reframing

After things go wrong, probably one of the most frequent questions that comes up when parents consider making things right is "Do I need to apologize to my kid?" There is no problem with saying a simple "I'm sorry," particular to older teenagers. What younger children, tweens, and even teens seem to relate to more strongly, however, is our ability to regroup, self-reflect, and speak with warmth and clarity about what went wrong and what we were trying to express. For example, after *once again* picking up your twelve-year-old son's shoes and putting them where they belong, you begin to lose it when he walks by and dumps his schoolbag on the floor next to you. Just as the contents tip over onto the floor, your anger spills out onto him. The Three Stooges of verbal communication—"you," "always," and "never"—are peppered throughout your accusatory out-burst. It's definitely not an elegant or attractive moment.

Here is a doable way to give yourself the space to make the repair. First you excuse yourself: "I'm not saying what I really mean. Just give me a moment." You walk into the next room, take a breath, and do what you now know how to do: you open your heart's arms to take in and assimilate the frustrations you are experiencing, then you breathe out your knowledge of your competence and centeredness. You do this maybe three times. It takes just a minute or two, perhaps longer if needed to feel that inner shift, the one that tells you that you have found your balance again.

You go into the kitchen, where your son is eating a spectacularly large bowl of cereal. You ask, "Are you okay?" He shrugs and nods yes. You begin, "All that I said when you got home? That really did come out wrong, and I did not mean to hurt your feelings. Obviously I was frustrated." He opens his eyes wide and stares into space, as if to say, "Oh, ye-e-s-s," but he has taken a break in his food demolition. You notice the look, but continue on: "It was not just about the bag or the shoes. It's been building up for a while because I feel like I am being taken for granted, and I know you don't mean to do that. What I meant to say was, I need a bit more cooperation about where you put your stuff." If it feels right, you might even go one step further: "And tonight after supper I really want to hear your plan. No long conversation needed, but we need to work this out."

The key sentences in this exchange are:

1. "That really did come out wrong, and I did not mean to hurt your feelings."
2. "What I meant to say was . . ."

What this course correction communicated and modeled to your son was that you had the ability to know when you had crossed a line and admit it. He also saw that by being willing to explore your emotions, you could be much more reasonable. Importantly, you modeled for your son that if you lose it, you don't have to justify and protect yourself; instead you can acknowledge you got it wrong and by doing so open a way to be clear about what was upsetting you and what you need. This is a pretty big life skill you just modeled. While saying a simple "Sorry, now let's put this behind us" might be another option, it can be too general, leaves things somewhat unresolved, and often does not have any depth of reflection, offer a chance to learn, or involve practical solutions.

In time, this kind of reframing can become a tool that feels familiar in your hand. Because you have been using the Compassionate Response Practice, two very significant options have opened up to you.

1. You can prevent yourself from being drawn into old patterns of even worse escalation because you have a healthy repair kit at hand, and all you have to do is create the space to access it.
2. You can now use the practice to recover and make repairs.

Sure, it would have been better not to have lost it, but rather than stand on either side of a relational chasm feeling lonely and ashamed, you have a dignified and genuine way to build bridges to your child that are natural and strong.

Coming Alongside

A lovely image for helping our children through their difficult times comes from the world of boating and canoeing. My colleague Todd Sarner first brought up the metaphor of "coming alongside." It describes what a canoe paddler will do for another who is in need of some help, by moving in beside the other boat to see what is needed. It implies that the two canoes are both going in the same direction and that no dramatic rescue is needed; it's more a gesture of "I am with you" or "I've got you."

The ability to come alongside implies that you are in control of your own vessel. It would serve little purpose to try to help if you were spinning out of control. What I hope this book has offered is this very crucial capacity to either proactively stay centered or regain your composure. Here is a list of coming-alongside skills and also what can happen if we get caught up in our own stuff.

1. Noticing the distress flare versus seeing only the flaws.

2. "I can see that something is upsetting you" versus "You always act like this when you are wrong."

3. Mother ship changes course versus doggedly continuing in the wrong direction.

4. "Let's see what's happening" versus "You never seem to understand!"

5. Moving in close versus barking instructions from a distance.

6. "Yes, it's hard when . . ." versus "Look, if you want to speak to me, you know where I am!"

7. Secure the line and tow into safe harbor versus rejecting or ignoring.

8. "Come sit near me. Can you help me understand?" versus "Just pull yourself together or go to your room!"

9. Make the repair versus ignoring the damage.

10. "So what do we need to do to make this work?"versus "Oh, come on, it's not that bad."

Remodeling

When there has been a blowup in the family, everyone is upset. Your child will likely be feeling vulnerable. As we discussed before, this kind of sensitivity can fast-track the repair, because when our kids are emotionally hurt, their radars are on high alert. We are all-powerful in this adult-child dynamic, and they are scanning us for clues about what will come next. It's a very primitive, brain-based survival strategy. They inwardly ask, "Will my mom get even madder?" or "Will my dad calm down?" If we can make even a tiny shift in our behavior by saying, with only a tinge of regret in our voice, "Oh. This is not coming out right. I need a moment," they *will* pick up that we have moved in the direction of at least not being scary, and their fight-or-flight response can begin to stand down.

When we use the Compassionate Response Practice, on one important level we are regulating our own nervous system. This will lead to coregulation, as your child now feels safe enough to open herself to absorbing and imitating your well-controlled emotions. In this sense we are, situation by situation, quite literally remodeling our own neurological responses as we train ourselves to move from an ancient survival mechanism to an ability to call on our collaborative brain centers. Over time our children will model their behavior on ours, and in doing so they will activate neurological pathways of empathy.

Standing on Your Own Ground

A young man who had not had an easy life was walking down a street when a group aggressively approached him, shouting profanities. The things they said were vulgar and very personal. The man looked at them and responded in a clear voice, tinged with just a little humor, "So tell me something about myself that I don't already know." A potentially dangerous situation was defused, and the young men went their own ways. There were many other choices this man could have made. But he had constructed his life with care and support, and he had explored his issues with a group of kind and skilled people. So when these shortcomings were thrown at him in the street, he was able to recognize them and stay centered. Most importantly—as his safety depended on it—he was able to recognize instinctively what he could and could not control. There was no way for him to stop the jeering group from saying disgusting things, but he could be in charge of the way he reacted. And he did just that.

Repairing attitudes and relationships is within your sphere of influence. No one can dissuade you from assimilating your worries, anxieties, and difficulties. No matter how challenging the situation, you are free to truly live into your brilliance, centeredness, and competence. You do it silently and powerfully. You cannot be easily coerced or bullied, because your ability takes the oxygen out of a situation that could otherwise have become inflamed. No one can manipulate you by prying open the cracks in your personality and exposing them. Why? Because you know your flaws all too well, and these shortcomings no longer prowl dangerously at the dark edge of your consciousness. You have shone a gentle but clear light on them, have worked mindfully to explore and assimilate them. This is not to say that anxieties and fears will not rise up ever again, but now you have a way to keep them in perspective. From time to time we meet people who have a "special something" that is hard to define; we come close to being able to put words to it when we say, "They know themselves." When *you* cultivate these qualities in yourself, the feeling of security, quiet confidence, and a growing sense of self-knowledge are palpable.

The Emotional Climate Control in Our Homes

Our moods and the way we deal with them affect much of our children's behavior. When we were single or before we had children, we could be sullen, and the only person it would disturb was us (those were the days!). Now, because we are in a family, it can seem like we are living in a constant and unrelenting emotional echo chamber, where our every utterance is picked up, amplified, and broadcast to the entire neighborhood and beyond. It was so funny when a dad once said, "When my daughter was young she was always checking me out. She would answer the phone and say politely, 'Yes, he is here, but he is being very grumpy.'" He went on, "Now she is a teenager, and she is pretty much still doing the same sort of thing, only now she can do it better and can be so much more embarrassing."

It can be a burden to always feel the responsibility to be kind and good. The Compassionate Response Practice gives you some realistic strategies to tune in to your grouchiness, accept it, and assimilate it; to recognize that you often are not dragged down by these feelings; and to keep the family energy moving before the mood goes viral.

Self-Forgiveness

Many times throughout this book we have explored the inextricable truth that parenting is a path of self-development unlike any other. There is no other aspect of life that brings together a dynamic collision between our tender dreams and cruel reality, our superpowers and gaping frailties, the endurance of an injured marathon runner determined to finish the race and the impatience of an unfortunately caffeinated New York City cabdriver. Most of all we experience selfless and helpless love with a depth of soul from which there is no rescue asked or given.

Each time we stumble, we are faced with the nagging possibility that we are somehow damaging our kids, and it feels awful. Self-doubting questions slink through our hearts: "Does he see how clueless I really am?" "Will she tell her friends stories about how I let her down?" "Will they grow up to resent me?" However, turning toward these fears and bringing them softly, but with confidence, into the light allows us to see them for what they really are: love's furnace and forge that we use to heat and hammer ourselves straight and strong. If we can allow this picture enough space to become a simple reality, when we yet again get it wrong with our child, something special happens. We find that we can forgive ourselves, knowing we now have the blacksmith's instruments to take the raw material of our imperfections and transform them into the tools we need to build a strong dwelling for our family.

Self-forgiveness does not come easily for a parent, and yet it is liberating to step out of the shadows of remorse and accept ourselves for the whole human beings we are. Flawed and gorgeous, we can quietly embrace both these aspects of ourselves, and in doing so we can stand on our own true ground and speak in our own true voice.

Conclusion

I hope my sharing of these heartfelt stories of the good, the bad, and the seemingly ordinary moments of family life has helped you feel less alone in your experience. As I set them down on these pages, I felt each one as a small gift that kind and caring people have given us. For parents in particular, these accounts can lead us out of the dark place of self-disappointment and creeping shame, show us how to laugh at our shared mishaps, and lead us to face another day with greater acceptance of our flaws and also appreciation for the beauty we create for our dear ones.

This is an unusual parenting book because the central theme has not focused on childhood. Rather, it has explored our adult world of emotional self-regulation as it relates to family life. It has allowed us the space to take a journey through our own inner landscape, which is something we do not often grant ourselves.

There is a good metaphor that seems to sum up our need to attend to our own development. It comes up every time I sit on board a plane, waiting to take off. I see the flight attendants go through their routine, telling us to put the oxygen mask on our face first before securing our child's. I sometimes wonder if the other people watching also see the direct relationship between the safety advice and what we need to do as parents in order to survive extreme turbulence and an emergency landing. I have to restrain myself from annoying my neighbor by saying something about how this metaphor is so true, because as parents the first thing we need to address is our own capacity to help our kids in order to be effective in securing them. But still, like a goofy child, I look forward to the safety announcement every time I fly. And every time, I respond to the reminder to first tend to my own oxygen with the promise "I will."

Appendix:
Verses to Prepare for the Compassionate Response Practice

Dear guardian being who keeps watch
Over my destiny.
Through the waking and sleeping,
And the long ages of time:

May my thoughts, filled with hope,
Reach deep into me through you.

May I be strengthened
From the founts of will
Which bear us towards freedom.

May I be illumined
From the founts of wisdom
Which warm the inmost heart.

May I feel peace
From the founts of love
Which bless our work.
—Adam Bittleston, "Intercessory Prayer (For One's Self)"
  Adapted from the original

———

Dear guardian being who keeps
Watch over the destiny of [*say the name of the child*]
Through the waking and
sleeping,
And the long ages of time:

May my thoughts, filled with
hope,
Reach this child through you.

May this child be strengthened
From the founts of will
Which bear us towards freedom.

May this child be illumined
From the founts of wisdom
Which warm the inmost heart.

May this child feel peace
From the founts of love
Which bless our work.
—Adam Bittleston, "Intercessory Prayer
  (For a Child in Need)"

May the events that seek me
Come unto me
May I receive them
With a quiet mind
Through the Father's ground of peace
On which we walk.

May the people who seek me
Come unto me
May I receive them
With an understanding heart
Through the Christ's stream of love
In which we live.

May the spirits who seek me
Come unto me
May I receive them
With a clear soul
Through the healing Spirit's Light
By which we see.
—Adam Bittleston, "Against Fear" from
  Meditative Prayers for Today

———

The wound is the place where the Light enters you.

Your acts of kindness are iridescent wings of divine love, which linger and continue to uplift others long after your sharing.

There is a life force within your soul, seek that life. There is a gem in the mountain of your body, seek that mine. O traveler,

if you are in search of that, don't look outside, look inside yourself and seek that.

You've seen my descent, now watch my rising.

Carry your baggage towards silence, when you seek the
signs of the way.

—Rumi

———

My bounty is as boundless as the sea,

My love as deep; the more I give to thee,

The more I have, for both are infinite.

—William Shakespeare, *Romeo and Juliet*

———

Come unto me, all you who labor and are heavy laden

and I will give you rest.

Take my yoke upon you, and learn of me;

for I am meek and lowly in heart

and I will give you rest unto your souls;

for my yoke is easy, and

my burden is light.

—Matthew 11:28–30

———

So we fix our eyes not on what is seen, but on what is unseen,

since what is seen is temporary, but what is unseen is eternal.

—Corinthians 4:16–18

———

God grant me the serenity

to accept the things I cannot change;

the courage to change the things I can;

and the wisdom to know the difference;

not my will, but your will be done.

—Reinhold Niebuhr, "Serenity Prayer"

———

The weak can never forgive. Forgiveness is the attribute of the strong.

—Mahatma Gandhi

———

Here I stand, I cannot do otherwise.

—Martin Luther

———

In the future no human being is to find peace in the enjoyment of others if others beside him are unhappy. . . . Every human being shall see in each and all of his fellow men a hidden divinity . . . that every human being is made in the likeness of the Godhead. When that time comes, every meeting between one man and another will of itself be in the nature of a religious rite, a sacrament.

—Rudolf Steiner, *The Work of the Angels*

———

We must eradicate from the soul all fear and terror of what comes out of the future.

We must acquire serenity in all our feelings and sensations about the future.

We must look forward with absolute equanimity to whatever may come.

And we must think only that whatever comes is given to us by world direction full of wisdom.

It is a part of what we must learn in this age, namely to live out of pure trust, without any security in existence, trusting in the ever present help of the spiritual world.

And we must seek this awakening within ourselves every morning and every evening.

—Rudolf Steiner, "Meditation for Courage"

———

No blame, no reasoning, no argument. Just understanding. If you understand, and show you understand, you can love, and the situation will change.

—Thich Nhat Hanh

———

I am not I

I am this one

Walking beside me, whom I do not see

Who at times I manage to visit

And at other times I forget

The one who forgives, sweet, when I hate

The one who remains silent when I speak

The one who is walking when I am not

The one who will remain upright when I die

—Juan Ramón Jiménez, "I Am Not I"

Bibliography

Chilton Pearce, Joseph. "Pregnancy, Birth, and Bonding." Touch the Future, 1984. https://ttfuture.org/files/2/members/sym_jcp_birth.pdf.

Coelho, Paulo. *The Devil and Miss Prym* [O Demônio e a Srta. Prym]. New York: HarperCollins, 2006.

Common Sense Media. "Landmark Report: U.S. Teens Use an Average of Nine Hours of Media Per Day, Tweens Use Six Hours." November 3, 2015. https://www.commonsensemedia.org/about-us/news/press-releases/landmark-report-us-teens-use-an-average-of-nine-hours-of-media-per-day.

Csikszentmihalyi, Mihaly. *Flow: The Psychology of Optimal Experience.* New York: HarperCollins, 1991.

Francis. *Gaudete Et Exsultate of the Holy Father Francis on the Call to Holiness in Today's World*. Libreria Editrice Vaticana, March 19, 2018. http://w2.vatican.va/content/francesco/en/apost_exhortations /documents/papa-francesco_esortazione-ap_20180319_gaudete-et -exsultate.html.

Henley, William Ernest. *A Book of Verses*. London: D. Nutt, 1888.

Herzog, Werner. Interview on *Fresh Air*. National Public Radio, October 29, 1998.

Kucinskas, Jaime, Bradley R. E. Wright, D. Matthew Ray, and John Ortberg. "States of Spiritual Awareness by Time, Activity, and Social Interaction." *Journal for the Scientific Study of Religion* 56, no. 2. (August 2017): 418–37.

Mintel Press Team. "The 'Rents Are Alright: Over Half (58%) of UK Children Say Their Parents Are Their Best Friends." Mintel Press Office, July 15, 2015. http://www.mintel.com/press-centre/social-and-lifestyle /the-rents-are-alright-over-half-58-of-uk-children-say-their-parents-are -their-best-friends.

Tsukayama, Hayley. "Teens Spend Nearly Nine Hours Every Day Consuming Media." *Washington Post*, November 3, 2015. https://www .washingtonpost.com/news/the-switch/wp/2015/11/03/teens-spend -nearly-nine-hours-every-day-consuming-media/?utm_term=.4dda c2c5b62e.

Williamson, Marianne. *A Return to Love: Reflections on the Principles of A Course in Miracles*. New York: HarperCollins, 1992, pp. 190–91.